It Works for Me with SoTL

A Step-by-Step Guide

By Hal Blythe, Charlie Sweet,
& Russell Carpenter

NEW FORUMS

NEW FORUMS PRESS INC.

Published in the United States of America
by New Forums Press, Inc.1018 S. Lewis St.
Stillwater, OK 74074
www.newforums.com

Copyright © 2017 by New Forums Press, Inc.

All rights reserved. No part of this publication may be reproduced or transmitted in any form or by any means, electronic or mechanical, including photocopy, or any information storage or retrieval system, without permission in writing from the publisher.

Library of Congress Cataloging-in-Publication Data Pending

This book may be ordered in bulk quantities at discount from New Forums Press, Inc., P.O. Box 876, Stillwater, OK 74076 [Federal I.D. No. 73 1123239]. Printed in the United States of America.

ISBN 10: 1-58107-307-0
ISBN 13: 978-1-58107-307-2

Table of Contents

Acknowledgements v
Preface vii
I. The Coming of Age of SoTL 1
II. The Best Two SoTL Articles We Ever Wrote..7
III. Theories of SoTL: An Overview 11
Part A. Historical Perspectives 12
    Designing Effective Cooperative Learning Workshops
        through Reflective Practice...12
    Understanding Cooperative, Collaborative, Problem-Based,
        and Team-Based Learning through the Scholarship of Integration 16
    Personal Retrospective on the Genesis of Cooperative Small Group
        Discovery Learning in Mathematics...19
    Personal Retrospective on a Lengthy Career with the Scholarship
        of Teaching and Learning (SoTL)..25

Part B. Theoretical Perspectives 39
    The Theoretical Framework: Gatekeeper to the Scholarship
        of Teaching & Learning 39
    Student-Faculty Collaboration in Higher Education...43
    The Fourth R, The Relationship Skills: Definition, Taxonomy,
        Procedures for Teaching, and Applications for Graduate Education 46
    Best Practice Teaching: What Individual and Contextual Variables
        Affect Who Adopts Best Practices Teaching Technology?...........................52

IV. Preparing to Create SoTL: An Overview 55
    Building Institutional Support for SoTL 56
    Try Out Your New Pedagogy. Find Out What Works. Share It
        with the World. Hold on! Not So Fast 58
    Navigating the IRB for SoTL Research: Guideline for the IRB Process...............60
    How SoTL Can Work for You..64
    Why Not Study Syllabi? Conduct High Quality Research
        on What You Already Know and Do...66
    Taking Steps to Control Variables in a Quantitative Quasi-Experiment...............67
    Research Support Faculty Fellow 69

Read and Replicate: Two Necessary Activities for Teaching
and SoTL Excellence 72
Faculty Book Group on the Scholarship of Teaching and Learning 73
Reflection as Transition Between Sequential Courses: The Focused
Autobiographical Sketch 76
A Blueprint to Encourage Student Writing 78
Teaching Tips as a Means of SoTL Scholarship: Yes, Write Some
Tips Like the Ones You Are Reading Now 81
SoTL-Based Best Practices for Creating Welcoming Classrooms
for Students of Color 83
Fostering an Environment of Discovery Through Discussion 85

V. Putting Theory into Practice: An Overview 87
Designing a SoTL Professional Learning Community (PLC)
Experience for Faculty Development 88
Getting Engaged in a SoTL Community: Project Syllabus
as an Example from Psychology 89
Transdisciplinary Faculty and Graduate Student Collaboration to Train
Our Future Teachers and Researchers: the Bailey Scholars Method 92
Lesson Study: A Means for Faculty Collaboration 94
Interdepartmental Faculty Collaboration 96
Interdisciplinary Peer Observation Groups 98
Evaluating the Long-Term Impact of Practicum Courses on Students 100
SoTL Works for Doctoral Students in Education 103
Projects for Business Students 105
Becoming Scholarly Teachers: Assigning a Pedagogical Strategy Paper
and Discussion Forum to Teach Doctoral Students about SoTL 107
Creating Online Presence: Weekly Video Feedback Brings
Everyone Together 109
How To Provide Students with Amazing and Awesome Feedback 113
Designing Online Faculty Development to Facilitate SoTL 115
Guide on the Side in the Form of a Text Message 119
The Graphical Gradebook 122
Reducing the Digital Divide at the Organizational Level 123

VI. My SoTL Project 127

VII. The Future of SoTL 135

About the Authors 137

Acknowledgements

For the tenth time, we want to thank the busy scholars from around the country who carved out time to contribute to this book. We also appreciate our publisher, Doug Dollar, for putting up with our constant onslaught of creativity and scholarship. Our award for the Most Contributions from a Single University again goes to Spalding University, where both Dede Wohlfarth and her colleague Nate Mitchell mentored the masses.

Preface

Like a lot of higher education instructors, Hal and Charlie ventured formally into the new field of the Scholarship of Teaching and Learning (SoTL) in the mid-1990s. By 1998 they had published *It Works for Me: Shared Tips on Teaching* (New Forums), and its sequel, *It Works for Me, Too: More Shared Tips for Effective Teaching,* appeared in 2002. Both books featured practical tips for teaching more than theory or research. From 2001 to 2011, they published a pedagogical piece in every issue of *Eureka Studies in Teaching Short Fiction* about concerns with effective instruction in literature (their home department back then was the Department of English & Theatre). Along the way, they also published "Total Team Teaching—Sharing Teaching Duties Equally" in *The Teaching Professor* in 2004 and numerous articles on the burgeoning field of creative writing.

Informally, they were practicing SoTL before Boyer called it the Scholarship of Teaching in 1990s *Scholarship Reconsidered*. Nonetheless, back in the 1970s they were producing pedagogical aids. For instance, unable to find and get permission to use a well-structured argument, they ended up writing a fictitious editorial against drunk driving (supposedly authored by one Olliver Bradley) that they claimed appeared in the pages of *The Woodhole Gazette*. Students were asked to examine the op ed piece for its use of thesis, issues (or claims), and evidence. They even turned their reflections on creative writing techniques into articles they sold to *Writer's Digest* and *The Writer*. In short, they were bringing pedagogy to a mass audience.

Significantly, they had realized that like a Venn diagram, teaching and scholarship, the two major parts of a professor's workload, intersected and that vast territory needed exploring. As more and more instructors come to the same perception, the need exists for a book that maps that territory and provides practical examples of how to successfully navigate it. The only way the young field of SoTL matures is if its participants share their ideas and develop a common language about the experience.

We are hopeful this book begins a conversation at the crossroads of the scholarly frame of mind and the pedagogical mindset. Every day in an era of shrinking funds and closer scrutiny by external forces enhancing the quality of instruction becomes more essential for the progress of higher education . . . perhaps its survival.

I. The COMING OF AGE OF SoTL

As we celebrate SoTL's 27th birthday (since Boyer's first sketchy attempt at a definition of this concept in 1990), we realize just how young the scholarship of teaching & learning really is. We are not only aware of how far the field has come in such a short time, but also the maturation issues SoTL must overcome to be fully accepted. Perhaps nothing rammed those challenges home so much as reading over the very wide variety of submissions for this book. We also had more questions from contributors to this book than we did for the first nine total, and all but one asked if something they proposed fit inside our definition of SoTL.

We are not alone in our assessment of the current state of SoTL. According to Cox, Huber, and Hutchings (2004), 90% of Carnegie Scholars agree or strongly agree that "confusion among faculty about what constitutes the scholarship of teaching and learning is an obstacle to greater involvement in the scholarship of teaching and learning at my institution" (p. 148). Despite this confusion, however, never before have so many SoTL publishing opportunities opened up. Kern, Mettetal, Dixson, and Morgan (2015) cite as support "the involvement of the Carnegie Foundation, the founding of several multidisciplinary journals devoted to the scholarship of teaching and learning, and increased interest on the part of many discipline-based professional organizations. In addition, organizations such as the International Society for the Scholarship of Teaching and Learning (ISSoTL) have been founded with missions exclusively devoted to SoTL" (p. 1). We have found somewhere around 100 pedagogical periodicals out there.

Establishing a Definition

Perhaps SoTL's number-one need at this moment, then, is not a birthday cake, but a clear definition that recognizes the vastness of the territory. In *Enhancing Scholarly Work on Teaching & Learning* (2006), Weimer defines not SoTL, but **pedagogical scholarship** as "published work on teaching and learning authored by college faculty in fields other than education" (p. 19). Weimer also limns such scholarship as existing on a pedagogical continuum from wisdom-of-practice scholarship to pure educational research. In a seminal article published in *Change* (1999), Hutchings and Schulman,

after attributing some of the definition confusion to Boyer's failure "to draw a sharp line between excellent teaching and the scholarship of teaching" (p. 13), list several characteristics of what they call "the scholarship of teaching" as being:
- "public";
- "open to critique and evaluation";
- "in a form others can build on"; and
- involving "question-asking, inquiry, and investigation, particularly around issues of student learning" (p. 13).

Hutchings and Schulman summarize these traits, claiming, "A scholarship of teaching is not synonymous with excellent teaching. It requires a kind of 'going meta,' in which faculty frame and systematically investigate questions related to student learning—the conditions under which it occurs, what it looks like, how to deepen it, and so forth—and do so with an eye not only to improving their own classroom but to advance practice beyond it" (p. 13).

Martin, Benjamin, Prosser, and Trigwell (1999) offer another angle of vision for their definition, believing the scholarship of teaching combines three related activities:
- Confronting extant teaching & learning knowledge;
- Metacognition about teaching and learning (but they believe, unlike us, it must be in one's discipline); and
- Public sharing (again within the discipline).

McKinney (2007) begins with a summation: "Perhaps most commonly shared are the notions of SoTL as involving some form of reflection on teaching and learning, and that this reflection or some product of the reflection is shared with peers" (p. 8). She also argues that SoTL 'shares established criteria of scholarship in general, such as that it is made public, can be reviewed critically by members of the appropriate community, and can be built upon by others to advance the field" (p. 12).

Another way of defining SoTL is to examine various work products designated as such. Secret, Leisey, Lannning, Polich, and Schaub (2011) conducted such a survey and determined the list included data-driven studies, case studies, reflective essays on teaching, literature reviews, and textbooks. Interestingly, developing course materials and blogging on teaching and learning were not as accepted.

Now it's our turn. Back in *It Works for Me as a Scholar-Teacher* (2008), we provided a summary of the essential traits of SoTL (p. 18), which we would like to amend. Generally speaking, SoTL pieces display these characteristics:
1. **Public**: SoTL has been published or presented in a public forum. As such, the author(s) has notified the world of participating in the scholarly conversation.

2. **Open**: No piece of SoTL seems so definitive as to shut the door on some other scholar piggybacking upon it. In fact, it invites others to build upon it and, like a Lego block, fit it into new configurations.
3. **Pedagogically tied to learning**: SoTL may involve a specific teaching technique, but it ties that piece to student learning.
4. **Utilizing an investigative process of discovery**: SoTL uses an organized method of inquiry, such as a problem to be solved, a practice to be analyzed, a question to be answered, or a theory to be investigated.
5. **Piggybacks**: Not only does SoTL invite piggybacking, but it demonstrates the piggybacking procedure itself. Starting with old knowledge, it develops new knowledge. It is scholarship that utilizes extant scholarship.
6. **Innovative**: SoTL admits the possibility that occasionally a practitioner might be struck by a bolt from the blue, perhaps an unexplained or unproven insight that is merely proffered for future development (n.b., this principle of innovation may be seen as an exception to many of the essential characteristics).
7. **Demonstrates expertise**: SoTL expertise might be not just in the subject under consideration, but in the very process or methodology being employed.
8. **Sourced**: Where applicable, SoTL notes its ancestry, demonstrating a knowledge of proper documentation and research techniques.
9. **Impactful**: Student learning is changed for the better from a small to a large degree.

But beyond its definition, the continuum of SoTL runs from wisdom-of-practice essays to educational research. The closer to research, the greater SoTL's value to the institution, but not necessarily to the practitioner. Thus, not all SoTL can be viewed or assessed the same, but that's an argument for another place.

Why SoTL, Why Now

As we enter a new era of academic accountability, state legislatures, the principle funders of many institutions, are scrutinizing every aspect of higher education, and their gaze has even fallen upon traditional academic scholarship, resulting in a series of tough questions seldom asked before. How many would read an essay on the triptych format of James Joyce's "Araby," and for those few perusers, how important would be the article be? How much influence would it have on literary studies, how much would it impact student learning, and, more importantly, how much time did it take the two writers of the piece to craft it for publication when they could have been teaching—or researching and writing about student learning? As Kern, Mettetal, Dixson, and Morgan (2015) assert,

"Both accreditation and state funding formulas are increasingly linked to evidence of student learning" (p. 10).

But it's not just pragmatic outside oversight. Promotion & Tenure as well as Merit Committees are asking a similar question: Does the product promote enhanced student learning? Even the writers of such a piece (in this case, us) need to ask themselves *cui bono* from such an article? Students' or professors' vitas? No one is advocating eliminating traditional research, but we are suggesting that the same amount of effort needed to produce one piece of literary criticism that dissolves behind the veil of esoterica could develop an article that can aid millions. Interestingly, while University Promotion & Tenure committees often find it difficult to evaluate pure disciplinary scholarship, such committees have little trouble understanding any faculty member's credentials that include SoTL.

As SoTL comes of age, then, an answer to those career-impacting questions from both inside and outside the academy becomes progressively clearer. SoTL demonstrates the same research skills as those needed to produce the Joyce article, but also provides the value added element of contributing to student learning. Additionally, SoTL can be performed at any institution without additional funding or use of scientific equipment in expensive labs. All it takes is a good idea, a willingness to create some sort of survey or assessment document, and the time to analyze it.

The good ideas become the easiest part of the SoTL equation. Every time you revise your syllabus, for instance, have you actually performed a SoTL study that supports the addition or deletion? As we have written about earlier (see our first collection in the *It Works for Me* series), years ago we decided to give quizzes in every class, undergraduate and graduate, every period. Even though we were fairly new to SoTL at that time, our decision to do so was not based on a whim. We had informally studied the grade differences between similar classes either given or NOT given quizzes as well as student comments on class evaluations. After our almost 40 years of classroom experience, the final piece of evidence to support our decision came recently as we researched the concept of retrieval.

Publishing SoTL can also increase your pedagogical skills. While your institution may not have a motto such as "Excellence in teaching is job one," we're sure it values good teaching. As Kern, Mettetal, Dixson, and Morgan (2015) assert, "engaging in SoTL would seem to encourage, but not guarantee, excellent teaching" (p. 9). After noting that "There is no relationship between research and teaching" (p. 169), Weimer (2006) emphasizes that "Doing pedagogical research does make you a better teacher" and offers several reasons for the assertion:

- You explore the questions that interest you.
- You develop instructional awareness.

- You think more deeply about teaching and learning.
- You improve for the right reasons.
- Your teaching stays fresh over the long haul.
- Your conversations with colleagues improve (actually become more evidence-based).
- It fosters learning in new ways from new people (p. 170).

As Kern, Mettetal, Dixson, and Morgan (2015) argue, "SoTL may be the broadest application of the Boyer model in that it often involves all four of Boyer's scholarships" (p. 7). As such, what better way can a scholar demonstrate to a P&T committee the ability to apply all four Boyer types of scholarship?

SoTL benefits institutional assessment and administrative work for those scholars in leadership positions.

Perhaps the major gap in most university professors' training involves the area of teaching. Research has shown that most encounter so little pedagogical materials in their doctoral programs, often train in programs that have no teaching assistantships available, and rarely attend purely pedagogical conferences. Then these newly-minted Ph.Ds are thrown into the classroom where their career's fate will be decided. Successfully understood and pursued, SoTL can help fill this important gap in their education, allowing for career advancement and deeper student learning.

Why SoTL? Why not!

References

Blythe, H. & Sweet, C. (2008). *It Works for Me as a Scholar-Teacher*. Stillwater, OK: New Forums.

Boyer, E. (1990). *Scholarship reconsidered: Priorities of the professoriate*. San Francisco, CA: Jossey-Bass.

Cox, R., Huber, M. T., & Hutchings, P. (2004). *Survey of CASTL scholars*. Stanford, CA: The Carnegie Foundation for the Advancement of Teaching.

Hutchings, P. & Schulman, L. (1999). The Scholarship of teaching and learning: New elaborations, new developments. *Change, 31*(5), 10-15.

Kern, B., Mettetal, G., Dixson, M., & Morgan, R. (2015). The role of SoTL in the academy: Upon the 25th anniversary of Boyer's *Scholarship reconsidered*. *Journal of the Scholarship for Teaching and Learning, 15*(3), 1-14.

Martin, E., Benjamin, J., Prosser, M. & Trigwell, K. (1999). Scholarship of teaching: A study of the approaches of academic staff, PPS. 326-331. In C. Rust (Ed.), *Improving student learning: Improving student learning outcomes*. Oxford, MA: Oxford Centre for Staff Learning and Development, Oxford Brookes University.

McKinney, K. (2007). *Enhancing learning through the scholarship of teaching and learning.* Bolton, MA: Anker.

Secret, M., Leisey, M., Lanning, S., Polich, S., & Schaub, J. (2011). Faculty perceptions of the scholarship of teaching and learning: Definition, activity level and merit considerations at one university. *Journal of the Scholarship of Teaching and Learning, 11*(3), 1-20.

Weimer, M. (2006). *Enhancing scholarly work on teaching & learning.* San Francisco, CA: Jossey-Bass.

II. The Best Two SoTL Articles We Ever Wrote

Not all writing is planned for in advance. Sometimes, in fact, if you don't take the opportunity to try to figure something out by writing about it—i.e., writing for discovery—solutions will continue to evade you. Sometimes, to get where you want to go, you have to write it out.

Article One

A case in point is one of the best SoTL articles we ever wrote. We were not planning to write it and probably would never have crafted it had not a happy accident occurred. In late 2008 we received an email from our predecessor as director of our Teaching & Learning Center. Doug had moved on to another university and was currently acting as an editor for the POD network, an organization that had agreed to supply the *NEA Higher Education Advocate* with material for a section of their journal under the general heading of "Thriving in Academia." Doug was in a bind—a person who had agreed to write the next column had pulled out. Could we, Doug wondered one Monday morning, write a piece following the journal's format, and could we have it complete by Friday?

Writing on demand was not the problem. We had spent the previous 25 years producing an article a year for popular creative writing magazines such as *Writer's Digest* and *The Writer*. We'd even done a monthly column on writing for *Byline* and, more importantly, been the ghost writers for one Brett Halliday novella for each month's *Mike Shayne Mystery Magazine*.

The problem was the SoTL subject. About what topic could we write 2500 words? Was there anything we were doing, researching, or even putting on workshops about that could supply us with grist for Doug's mill?

At around the same time we had taken over leadership of the University's New Faculty Orientation (NFO), where we spent an entire morning with incoming teachers facilitating a workshop on pedagogy since teaching would be the newbies' primary responsibility. We were also formalizing a new classroom observation service for all faculty, and one of the things that struck us about the teachers was their lack of organization. In fact, we clearly recall looking at an instructor's classroom evaluations and one sentence jumping out at us—"We never knew where we were."

That germ started our brainstorming. In our NFO workshop we were familiar with the research that demonstrated professors considered their number-one problem to be organization. Aha! All we had to figure out was an organizing pattern that would be appropriate for each class session, no matter the methodology the instructor used.

A year earlier we had helped the University write its Quality Enhancement Program (QEP) theme on critical and creative thinking. We then founded the QEP Coaches, a group tasked with developing critical and creative thinking skills among faculty and students. To help us with workshops, we brought in Buffalo State's Gerry Nosich, who wrote an extremely important book, *Learning to Think Things Through: A Guide to Critical Thinking across the Curriculum* (2001). Gerry's central insight is that students cannot learn everything in a textbook, so the most important thing an instructor can do is teach just "the fundamental and powerful concepts." Note we just did what Gerry taught us.

Synchronistically, we had just read a book we found reviewed in the *Wall Street Journal*. Chip and Dan Heath's *Made to Stick* (2007) analyzed political and advertising campaigns in order to discover "the core of the idea." At the end of their book they had distilled their formula for successful communication—whether in advertising, political campaigns, or similar endeavors—into an acronym, SUCCESS. Synthesizing our research told us we needed to come up with not only an organizational scheme for good classroom teaching, but also an acronym that would make that organization stick.

First, we performed a fast literature review on the subject (made easier by our Center having so many books), and gradually we began to whittle down the pedagogical research on organization into five major principles. On Day 2 we started writing, and suddenly the desired acronym snapped into focus:

1. **C**ontextualize: announce the new fundamental and powerful concept (FPC) around which everything else revolves.
2. **R**eview: tie this new FPC to recent old knowledge.
3. **I**terate: continually emphasize the FPC in various forms (examples).
4. **S**ummarize: finish class with a succinct summary of the FPC and attendant concepts.
5. **P**review: give students specific directions on what they need to be looking for in the assignment for the next class.

The acronym C.R.I.S.P. came fairly easily, though we had to search our thesaurus for "Iterate." Like *Wheel of Fortune* contestants, we needed a vowel somewhere.

For the rest of the article we utilized the research (e.g., Brookfield's *The Skillful*

Teacher, *McKeachie's Teaching Tips*, *Made to Stick*, and Nosich's book). We supplemented that research with examples taken from Charlie's favorite American Literature class. By Friday, we had our final draft of the article sent off to Doug, and "Keeping Your Classroom C.R.I.S.P.: Unity of Purpose as an Organizing Principle" was published in December 2008 in the *NEA Higher Education Advocate* (26.2, pp. 5-8).

Perhaps our greatest insight from the researching and writing of this SoTL article is embodied in the old coaches' saying, "Pressure builds diamonds." In short, we found we functioned better under pressure. Knowing we had a deadline and Doug was counting on us drove us to produce an excellent article. Since then, we have found that without deadlines, self-imposed or given to us, we don't work as well. In fact, this month as we have been writing and editing this book, we are also finishing a book on scholarship for New Forums and the sixth novel in our Clement County Saga series, and last year we published six books as well as a weekly blog, four columns for the *National Teaching & Learning Forum*, and a couple of other articles.

Article Two

Our second such article came about out of necessity. We'd completed major SoTL projects focused on developing better understandings of our Minor in Applied Creative Thinking. SoTL allows scholars to see teaching (their own and the pedagogies of others) differently and in ways not available in pure assessment. We launched the minor to give our students a competitive advantage on the job market.

One of the most memorable and revealing SoTL research projects we undertook related to the minor focused on an examination of our introductory or gateway course—CRE 101, Introduction to Applied Creative Thinking. This course is popular among students from many different majors and at all levels. It fills quickly each semester it's offered.

The CRE 101 course establishes a foundation in creative thinking through instruction in basic theories and practices. Students will develop fluency in basic language and fundamental and powerful concepts of creativity studies. Students pursuing the minor in Applied Creativity must earn a C or above in this course. According to the syllabus, upon completion of the course, students will:

- Create effective creative products based on inquiry such as class discussion, critical analysis, integrative collaboration, observing, and using technology.
- Evaluate materials relevant to creative works discussed, presented, and created in this course.
- Analyze strategies for creative product and communication design.
- Apply effective strategies for integrative collaboration with team members to develop an effective creative project, product, or practice.

- Apply the design of the creative process to educational experiences and the creative endeavor generally.
- Demonstrate knowledge of the basic vocabulary and concepts of creativity study.

Rusty taught it for the first time several years ago and the second time in the subsequent semester. Hal and Charlie visited the class multiple times to observe, provide feedback, try lessons along with students, and co-facilitate discussion. The course lends itself to collaboration and generative thinking, which made it the ideal course to incorporate into a SoTL project.

Rusty taught the course twice, once using a traditional but reliable method aligned with seminars many of us took in college. Classes focused on discussion. Students might debrief about homework or questions they were to consider before coming to class. It was a good way to launch the course and learn from the students and faculty colleagues. Students responded well to the course as determined by standard evaluations at our institution.

The next semester he taught the course, Rusty decided to use a flipping approach. That is, students completed readings, assignments, and discussions online using the Learning Management System (LMS). Class time focused on collaborative, active learning. The primary question in this pedagogical shift, of course, is student learning. In this case, we were limited to student perception of learning. Flipped classes are, at times, considered more work, as class time requires thoughtful preparation and design, rather than lecture or book-based discussion. Interestingly, the students responded better to the flipped CRE 101 course. The class sessions were more focused on what the students needed to take away rather than instructor-focused. The SoTL methodology was simple—two courses, different pedagogical approaches. It's also replicable in other courses within the minor. In this case, however, the process and results provided plenty to consider as we continue to build the program. "Flipping the Creativity Class: Creating Active-Learning Environments for Student Innovations" was featured in *Best Practices for Flipping the College Classroom,* edited by Julee B. Waldrop and Melody A. Bowdon and published by Routledge, 2015: 118-130.

Conclusion

Notice in both cases we weren't planning on writing the article, but we were always aware of things occurring in our surroundings. Sometimes those things call out to us, demanding to be heard, requiring a fuller explanation. We admit we may drive ourselves crazy writing so much, but without a full plate, we don't thrive well in academia.

III. Theories of SoTL: An Overview

While this book, like the other nine in our *It Works for Me* series, focuses on actual SoTL examples and some tips for creating them, we open with a larger-than-normal section on SoTL theory. Not only did we receive some superb theoretical essays on SoTL, but we think it important to provide a more extnsive overview of a fairly new subject in academia.

Yet, SoTL is not quite as new as we thought. As with our previous book in this series, *It Works for Me, Metacognitively*, we were privileged to receive some contributions from old friends who are giants in the SoTL field (as well as other fields). Neil Davidson, Barbara Millis, and Richard Solomon once again illustrate the power of collaborative writing with their useful insights.

We have broken this Theory section into **Historical Perspectives** and **Theoretical Perspectives**. We are proud to act as an historical archive for the above-named trio. Neil Davidson's essay, in particular, provides an historic context to SoTL, for as Neil told us, he was doing SoTL twenty-five years before SoTL was called SoTL. We hope you enjoy it and the other introductory essays as much as we did.

Part A. Historical Perspectives

Designing Effective Cooperative Learning Workshops through Reflective Practice

Like most experts in the field of faculty development, I have been heavily influenced by concepts sometimes referred to as "reflective practice." Thinking about one's experiences to promote positive changes goes back at least as far as John Dewey (1933) and has modern advocates in Stephen Brookfield (1990, 1995), Donald Schon (1987) and others. Thus, in designing faculty development workshops, I am continually taking into account quantitative and qualitative feedback from faculty participants in earlier workshops, from colleagues who provide critiques and suggested changes, and from my own knowledge of educational theory and human dynamics. I always consider workshops "works in progress." As should be obvious, such an approach relates to the scholarship of teaching and learning—particularly because I deliberately publish my workshop practices (Millis, 2016, 2014, 2010, 2009).

My workshops on cooperative learning, a popular topic, are carefully crafted and always continuously revised. I deliberately build in and coordinate two key elements: (1) the workshop content and (2) the workshop execution. The workshop content on cooperative learning incorporates two features: practical procedures and group activities that faculty can immediately apply to their own courses and direct references to theories related to cooperative learning that tell faculty why and when to use these group activities. The workshop execution—how it is delivered—directly involves engaging the faculty participants in the activities themselves, not merely lecturing about them, and modeling these activities and the related classroom management procedures that support them. Additionally, the workshop execution also requires an essential yet somewhat "intangible" element: a passionate commitment to the cooperative learning content intended to positively inspire and motivate the participants.

Let me illustrate how these five key elements—practical activities, theory, active participation, modeling, and enthusiastic delivery— meld in a three-hour beginning workshop on cooperative learning. When these five elements are present, I usually accomplish two critical goals: First, faculty know not only what to do but also how to do it, and second, faculty have the confidence and the inspiration to attempt these often new teaching approaches.

The workshop begins with a brief overview of the goals and the agenda and then moves rapidly into a cartoon series projected to the entire group. These cartoons help to establish rapport by relaxing the audience and by making key points in a humorous, non-threatening way. Selected cartoons emphasize that, despite my focus on cooperative learning (structured group work), I am not "lecture-bashing"—indeed, the lecture can play a key role in teaching and learning. However, subsequent cartoons suggest that if teachers ONLY lecture, the research is clear: students will not retain/learn most of what is covered. I emphasize through two light-hearted cartoons that using group work to engage students provides an enlightened approach to teaching and can be fun for both teachers and students. This opening segment, which lays the groundwork for the workshop, takes ten minutes or less. I then go briefly into the just-discussed "lecture mode" by presenting seven key principles of cooperative leaning (Millis, 2002). This mini-lecture (ten minutes) gives faculty members some key theory that will help them put the upcoming group activities into perspective.

I introduce the first activity—a "Three-step Interview"—by getting students first into pairs and then into groups of four through interviews. Person A interviews person B, and then they switch roles, B interviewing A, using the same content-related questions: "How familiar are you with cooperative learning? To what extent do you use it in your classes? In what ways?" In the third step, two pairs unite, with each person introducing his or her partner to the foursome, explaining how their partner uses cooperative learning. As the activity and the later debriefing session unfolds, I both model and discuss certain key classroom management strategies: (1) Use, if desired, a quiet signal to gain students' attention; (2) Explain the upcoming activity before commencing it; (3) Introduce a "sponge" or "extension" activity with a content-centered focus for pairs or groups that complete the original activity to move onto; and (4) Monitor (listen to) the participants as they interact. In addition to emphasizing these four classroom management procedures, the debriefing segment explores the uses and values of the Three-step Interview as well as giving some concrete examples.

As the faculty participants complete the Three-step Interview, I distribute group file folders containing a tent card, playing cards, and a sheet of paper for the upcoming activities. I explain the value of using team folders as a classroom management tool for collecting and distributing homework and activity materials. Each team displays a tent card identifying them, for example, as "Team Two, Team, Three," etc. The members of each team receive a playing card that provides an individual identity based on the suit: hearts, diamonds, spades, and clubs. Thus, a participant might serve as the three of diamonds or the four of hearts (the diamond within Team Three or the heart within Team Four).

Next I begin a second activity, "Roundtable," a cooperative learning structure useful for brainstorming, reviewing, predicting, or practicing a skill. Using the single sheet of paper in each team folder, the faculty participants write and say aloud one response to an open-ended question before passing the paper to the person on their left. The open-ended question they address is: What are some barriers to engaging students through cooperative activities? Your own misgivings? Student concerns? Departmental barriers? Institutional limitations? Typical barriers include faculty inexperience with group work, students' refusals to participate, and fixed chairs in auditoriums.

To keep faculty participants engaged and to bring closure, I next introduce a report-out method called "Stand Up and Share." The participants review the lists they just generated, making certain that any group member is able to serve as the spokesperson or reporter. I then call out a suit, and the person holding that card in each team rises with the Roundtable results. Rotating rapidly in sequential order, the spokespersons call out one barrier to cooperative learning, crossing it off their list. At some point, I call out another suit, and the reporters change.

As should be obvious, I have been modeling the use of folders as a source of the workshops materials, the use of tent cards to identify various teams, and the use of playing cards to designate individual team members. I also model through an enthusiastic delivery and my own course-related examples, my commitment to the approaches I am modeling. Feedback from former participants encourages me to remain open nevertheless to suggestions and concerns.

For the concluding activity, "Numbered Heads Together," each team identifies from their list a barrier they would like to solve. As a sponge activity, they select a second one. The teams then generate all the solutions they can think of for the given barriers, making certain that all team members understand and can explain the solutions if called upon to be the spokesperson. Because the reporters are not pre-identified, all participants want to know the material, often requesting coaching from their peers to bring them up-to-speed. I then use a report-out method called "Luck of the Draw," pulling various cards and having the matching spokespersons deliver their team's report. This process continues until time elapses. I emphasize that the Stand-up and Share activity followed the same approach as modeled here: In both cases, because the spokesperson is not pre-identified, all members want to be prepared to report on the completed task, thus encouraging peer coaching.

The workshop concludes with a cartoon review of key reminders about cooperative learning.

References

Brookfield, S. D. (1990). *The skilful teacher*. San Francisco, CA: Jossey-Bass

Brookfield, S. D. (1995). *Becoming a critically reflective teacher*. San Francisco, CA: Jossey-Bass.

Dewey, J. (1933). *How we think: A restatement of the relation of reflective thinking to the educative process* (1910), revised edition. Boston, MA: Heath.

Millis, B. J. (2016). Using metacognition to promote learning. *IDEA Paper #63*. Available at http://www.ideaedu.org/Portals/0/Uploads/Documents/IDEA%20Papers/IDEA%20Papers/PaperIDEA_63.pdf

Millis, B. J. (2014). Using cooperative structures to promote deep learning. *Journal on Excellence in College Teaching, 25*(3 & 4), 139-148.

Millis, B. J., Ed. (2010). *Cooperative learning for higher education faculty: Across the disciplines, across the academy*. Sterling, VA: Stylus.

Millis, B. J. (Spring 2009). Becoming an effective teacher using cooperative learning: A personal odyssey. *Peer Review: Emerging Trends and Key Debates in Undergraduate Education, 11*(2), 17-21. Available at http://www.aacu.org/peerreview/pr-sp09/pr-sp09_millis.cfm

Millis, B. J. (2002).Enhancing learning—and more!—through cooperative learning. *IDEA Paper #38*. Available at http://www.ideaedu.org/Portals/0/Uploads/Documents/IDEA%20Papers/IDEA%20Papers/IDEA_Paper_38.pdf

Schon, D. A. (1987). *Educating the reflective practitioner: Toward a new design for teaching and learning in the professions*. San Francisco, CA: Jossey-Bass.

Barbara Millis, director at four teaching and learning centers (retired)
   With editing input from:
Neil Davidson, University of Maryland, Professor Emeritus
Richard Solomon, University of Maryland (retired)

Understanding Cooperative, Collaborative, Problem-based, and Team-based Learning through the Scholarship of Integration

In the past few decades, many higher education instructors have moved away from sole reliance on lectures toward instructional approaches in which, much of the time, students are active participants in the learning process.

Several approaches to foster active learning involve small group work, including cooperative and collaborative learning and more recently problem-based and team-based learning. Three of these four approaches are now deemed "evidence-based instructional practices" (i.e., causal research has shown that cooperative, problem-based, and team-based learning do indeed have a positive influence on student learning).

The benefit of the range of approaches is that teachers have multiple forms of group learning from which to choose. The challenge is that making a choice can be daunting, and at times, it can be difficult to distinguish among variations of group-learning approaches.

The four major forms of group learning share important elements. All four stand against passive modalities and lengthy lectures and use small group work as the means to achieve active learning (Bonwell & Eison, 1991). In addition, they have similar goals for teaching and learning, to encourage development of content knowledge and related intellectual skills.

The four approaches came from different origins and developed separately. Initially, advocates of the different approaches were unaware of each other. Each movement had its own turf and seemed happy remaining there.

Many educators have asked intriguing comparison questions about these approaches. Is collaborative learning a special form of cooperative learning, or vice-versa? Are problem-based learning or team-based learning variations of cooperative or collaborative learning, both, or neither? Confusion on these issues abounds in the literature.

The problem with such confusion is that we think we are talking about, doing, and researching the same thing, when in many cases, we are not (Weimer, 2014). This error in judgment has negative implications not only for research and development but also for the day-to-day practices of higher education instructors. Indeed "clarity" and "appropriate methods" are features of excellence in the scholarships of discovery, application, integration, or teaching (Glassick et al 1997; Boyer, 1990). The scholarship of integration involves "making connections across the disciplines, placing the specialties in larger context, illuminating data in a revealing way…" (Boyer 1990, 18-19).

Our project is an example of the scholarship of teaching and learning (SoTL) carried out through the scholarship of integration. In a special double issue of a journal, the key characteristics and important similarities and differences among the four small group instructional approaches are identified for the first time in a single volume (Davidson, Major, and Michaelsen 2014). We accomplish this analysis through two major synthesis articles, plus three articles apiece on cooperative learning, collaborative learning, problem-based learning, and team-based learning. The articles are written by experts in each of the four approaches, from different disciplines.

The Syntheses

The first synthesis, by Davidson and Major, highlights the similarities and differences among cooperative, collaborative, and problem-based learning. We provide definitions of the three approaches and describe essential features of each, specific strategies and techniques, and pertinent research. We also identify a set of common attributes among the small group approaches.

The second synthesis, by Michaelsen, Davidson, and Major, is entitled, "Team Based Learning Practices and Principles in Comparison with Cooperative Learning and Problem Based Learning." This article describes key characteristics of Team-Based Learning, and highlights how the other methods, cooperative learning and PBL, are similar and different from it.

What We Found: The Four Approaches in Brief

Cooperative learning is based on an educational philosophy such as Dewey's and on research in social psychology and group dynamics. Common elements among cooperative learning models include these: a task or learning activity suitable for group work, small-group interaction focused on the learning activity, interdependence in working together, cooperative and mutually helpful behavior among students, and individual accountability and responsibility.

Additional elements vary among cooperative learning models. For example, teachers can play an active role in building community, organizing the groups, and fostering interdependence. They might choose to assign roles or employ structured procedures such as the interview, think-pair-share, jigsaw, or group investigation.

Collaborative learning is based on the philosophy of social Constructivism. It intends to create an environment that helps an individual to develop mentally, emotionally, and socially as an active participant in a supportive learning community. Students work together in small groups that are typically self-selected, self-managed, and loosely structured. The teacher offers limited guidance so that students can develop their own independence. There are very few techniques specific to collaborative learning.

In problem-based learning, complex, real-world problems are used to motivate students to identify and research the concepts and principles needed to work through and solve the problems. Students work in learning teams (each of which typically has a trained facilitator), bringing together collective skill in acquiring, communicating, and integrating information. In PBL students are expected to think critically and be able to analyze and solve complex, real-world problems; find, evaluate, and use appropriate learning resources; work cooperatively in teams and small groups; and demonstrate versatile and effective communication skills, both verbal and written.

Team-based learning (TBL) places the focus on students actively engaging in activities that require them to *use* concepts to solve problems. Every aspect of a TBL course is specifically designed to foster the development of self-managed learning teams. Four foundational practices are essential for implementing TBL. These are: 1) strategically forming permanent teams, 2) ensuring student familiarity with course content by utilizing a Readiness Assurance Process, 3) developing students' critical thinking skills by using carefully-designed, *in-class* activities and assignments, and 4) creating and administering a peer assessment and feedback system.

It is illuminating to step back and consider the relationships among these approaches. Doing so enables us to learn from one another, and perhaps consider opportunities for working together. In addition, what makes our work unique is its invitation to practitioners to cross traditional boundaries and to begin productive conversations that can advance the field of small group learning.

In the spirit of learning together, we offer the following suggestions:

What cooperative learning might learn from collaborative learning: Teachers don't have to keep tightly structuring everything, especially after students develop some skill in group work.

What collaborative learning might learn from cooperative learning: Teachers can't assume that students have skills in working together; some of them don't. Be prepared to teach some social skills occasionally as needed.

What cooperative and collaborative learning might learn from PBL: Real world problems can form a foundation for meaningful and productive group work.

What PBL might learn from cooperative and collaborative learning: There are many interesting, meaningful, and productive learning assignments other than real-world problems; variety in tasks is the spice of life in groups.

What cooperative and collaborative learning might learn from TBL: a structured system of assessment quizzes motivates students to prepare for class by learning basic information outside of class through reading, listening, or viewing.

References

Boyer, E. L. (1990). *Scholarship reconsidered: Priorities of the professoriate.* Princeton, NJ: Carnegie Foundation for the Advancement of Teaching.

Davidson, N., Major, C., & Michaelsen, L. (Eds). (2014). Small-group learning in higher education – Cooperative, collaborative, problem-based, and team-based learning. *Journal on Excellence in College Teaching, 25*(3 & 4).

Glassick, C. E., M. T. Huber, & G. I. Maeroff. (1997). *Scholarship assessed: Evaluation of the professoriate.* San Francisco, CA: Jossey-Bass.

Weimer, M. (2014). Does it matter what we call it? *The Teaching Professor, 28*(3), 4.

Neil Davidson, University of Maryland, Professor Emeritus
Claire Howell Major, University of Alabama
Larry K. Michaelsen, University of Central Missouri.

Personal Retrospective on the Genesis of Cooperative Small Group Discovery Learning in Mathematics

In telling my story, I would like to acknowledge several professors who had a great impact on me. As a graduate student in pure mathematics, I had published just one mathematical research paper (Davidson and Fabian, 1963). Then the University of Wisconsin hired John G. Harvey to create a new doctoral program in mathematics education within the Mathematics Department. Doctoral students would take all their coursework and comprehensive exams in mathematics and then go on to take additional courses in education (first taught by Tom Romberg) and write a dissertation in mathematics education. I jumped at the chance to join that program.

In the mid-1960s at the University of Wisconsin, I was looking for a dissertation topic. I had taken several graduate mathematics courses taught by the Moore method (Moise, 1965) – my initial courses through Edward Fadell. This individualistic, competitive approach to math instruction led to spectacular successes in mathematical research for some, and discouragement for many others.

Dewey's (1916, 1938) philosophy of education, as taught by Donald Arnstine at the University of Wisconsin, emphasized learning through active personal experience; learning by doing non-routine, thought-provoking activities; learning as a social process; intrinsic motivation; and more. Dewey wrote, "The primary source of social control resides in the very nature of the work done as a social enterprise in which all individuals have an opportunity to contribute and to which all feel a responsibility." (1938, p. 56).

I was fortunate to stumble into a course in theories of social change, taught by David Bradford, employing small group processes in learning and presenting psychological research findings: Cooperation was superior to competition in groups (Deutsch, 1960). Democratic leadership was more effective than authoritarian or laissez-faire leadership (White and Lippitt, 1960). Group size affected discussions (Bales and Borgatta, 1961). Conformity pressure was a risk in groups, and it could be reduced (Asch, 1960).

Incorporating Dewey's philosophy, I aimed to retain the intellectual discovery challenge of the Moore method of math instruction, yet adding research-based social support in small groups to foster success for most students.

The SoTL aspects of this triple combination involved the scholarships of integration and of application. Selected ideas from each part of the combination were applied in designing the "small group discovery method."

I conducted a pilot study in 1966-67 and my dissertation study in 1967-68 in calculus for 12 brave students meeting 5 days per week for the academic year. Students working together cooperatively in small groups discussed mathematical ideas, developed techniques for solving problems, made conjectures for investigation, proved theorems, and discovered many ideas and techniques which were new to them. (Davidson 1970, 1971 a, b).

A class period typically began with a meeting of the entire class to provide an overall perspective. This process can include presenting new material, holding class discussions, posing problems or questions for investigation, and clarifying directions for the group activities.

The class is then divided into small groups, typically with four members apiece. Each group has its own working space, which might include a flipchart or section of the chalkboard. Students work together cooperatively in each group on challenging activities. They actively exchange ideas with one another and help each other learn the material.

Varied leadership and management functions are handled by the teacher: initiate group work, form groups, and present guidelines to foster cooperation and mutual helpfulness.

The teacher takes an active role, circulating from group to group, providing assistance and encouragement with learning and group process, and asking thought-provoking questions as needed.

Teachers furnish overall classroom management, tie ideas together, make assignments, and evaluate student performance.

The teacher presents to students the following guidelines for group problem solving (Davidson 1970, 1990):

- Work together in groups of four.
- Cooperate with other group members.
- Achieve a group solution for each problem.
- Make sure that everyone understands the solution before the group goes on.
- Listen carefully to others and try, whenever possible, to build upon their ideas.
- Share the leadership of the group.
- Make sure that everyone participates and no one dominates.
- Take turns writing problem solutions on the board.
- Proceed at a pace that is comfortable for your own group. (Don't race with other groups to see who is fastest.)

In the original study, students in the experimental group scored slightly higher but not significantly higher on a standard final exam than students in a lecture control group. (To attain significant differences in future cooperative discovery studies, I recommended that researchers also provide opportunities for students to practice and master the discovered facts and skills; this action is often neglected in discovery studies.)

Student attitudes toward learning and the course were overwhelmingly positive. Here are some sample statements from the original course and many other following courses: "Other students, no matter who, force you to learn more." "Most classes stress being able to use formulas while this stresses total understanding." "It is my most interesting and liked class. I enjoy coming to it." "I think I learned a lot more tis year than in all three years of high school math." "It showed me that I can do things that before looked impossible. All it takes is a little understanding. Math doesn't scare me as much now."

In other SoTL initiatives, further development of small group cooperative learning in mathematics occurred over many years. For example, one paper was a theoretical comparison of the Moore method and the small group discovery method (Dancis and Davidson, 1970). Motivational aspects of students in small group learning in mathematics were analyzed by Davidson (1976), with a framework of cognitive, ego-integrative, and social motives.

An overview of ten years of work with small group discovery was given by Davidson (1979). For a younger age group, Davidson, Agreen, and Davis (1978) presented techniques for small group learning in junior high mathematics.

A major professional association, the Mathematical Association of America, has published a number of journal articles (e.g. Davidson, 1971b; Weissglass, 1976; McKeen and Davidson, 1975). The latter one was a theoretical comparison of small groups versus individual instruction.

The MAA also published several major books related to cooperative learning in mathematics. A volume by Rogers, Reynolds, Davidson, and Thomas (2002) arose through Project CLUME: Cooperative Learning in Undergraduate Mathematics Education. Earlier volumes by Hagelgans, Reynolds et al (1995) and by Dubinsky, Reynolds, and Mathews (1997) incorporated aspects of Davidson's work.

Other publications on small group learning in mathematics occurred through the National Council of Teachers of Mathematics (NCTM). Examples are those by Artzt and Newman (1990), Leikin and Zaslavsky (1999), and an NCTM Yearbook chapter by Davidson (1990b).

NCTM also published an article by Davidson, McKeen and Eisenberg (1973), creating a model for developing curriculum materials with student input. A teacher observes one small group at a time, grappling with a challenging concept or problem. Observations and input from one group lead to a refined activity for the next group...After 3 or 4 groups, the activity is polished into good form.

This process was used to develop a small group discovery course in abstract algebra (Davidson and Gulick, 1976). This course had previously been considered impervious to discovery learning.

I had the good fortune to work in a congenial and collegial mathematics education group at the University of Maryland. One of our major projects with faculty and graduate students was developing a course in mathematics for elementary teachers (UMMaP: Cole, Davidson, Fey, Henkelman et al, 1978). Several of our doctoral students wrote dissertations related to this course.

For limited excursions with SoTL into research on small group learning in mathematics, see a selective review by Davidson (1985) and a research overview by Davidson and Kroll (1991). Urion and Davidson (1992) summarized results of several empirical studies.

If this were a literature review, not a brief personal retrospective, I would include major works by many other authors -- my apologies for not having space to do so here.

In my 50-year career in SoTL with cooperative small groups, I have found that any topic in any mathematics course can be taught using substantial small group interaction – perhaps including some lecture/discussion. With cooperative small group discovery learning in mathematics, the classroom blossoms into a vital intellectual learning community of engaged, communicative, supportive, thoughtful learners.

During the past 25 years, my work has expanded beyond mathematics to include cooperative learning in general. That body of work is given in another essay in this volume.

References

Asch, S.E. (1960). Effects of group pressure upon the modification and distortion of judgments. In D. Cartwright & A. Zander (Eds.), *Group dynamics: Research and theory* (2nd Ed.). New York, NY: Harper & Row.

Bales, R.F. and Borgatta, E.F. (1961). Size of group as a factor in the interaction profile. In A. P. Hare, E. F. Borgatta, & R. F. Bales (Eds.), *Small groups, studies in social interaction.* New York, NY: Alfred A. Knopf.

Cartwright, D. & Zander, A. (1960). *Group dynamics: Research and theory* (2nd Ed.). New York, NY: Harper & Row.

Dancis, J. & Davidson, N. (1970). The Texas method and the small group discovery method. In *The legacy of R. L. Moore.* (online and on CD)

Davidson, N. (1970, 1971a). *The small discovery method of mathematics instruction as applied in calculus.* Doctoral dissertation: University of Wisconsin, Madison. Published in 1971 by the Wisconsin Research and Development Center for Cognitive Learning.

Davidson, N. (1971b). The small group discovery method as applied in calculus instruction. *American Mathematical Monthly*, August-September, 789-791.

Davidson, N. (1976). Motivation of students in small-group learning of mathematics. *Frostburg State College Journal of Mathematics Education, 11,* 1-18.

Davidson, N. (1979). The small-group discovery method: 1976-77. In J. Harvey & T. Romberg (Eds.), *Problem solving studies in mathematics.* Madison, WI: The Wisconsin Research and Development Center for Individualized Schooling.

Davidson, N. (1980). Small-group learning and teaching in mathematics: An introduction for non-mathematicians. In S. Sharan, P. Hare, C. Webb, & R. Hertz-Lazarowitz (Eds.), *Cooperation in education* (pp. 136-145). Provo, UT: Brigham Young University Press.

Davidson, N. (1985). Small-group learning in mathematics: A selective review of the research. In R. Slavin, et al. (Eds.), *Learning to cooperate, cooperating to learn.* New York, NY: Plenum Press.

Davidson, N. (Ed.) (1990). *Cooperative learning in mathematics: A handbook for teachers.* Menlo Park, CA: Addison-Wesley. (available through Dale Seymour).

Davidson, N. (1990). Small group cooperative learning in mathematics. In T. Cooney (Ed.), *Teaching and learning mathematics in the 1990s.* Reston VA: National Council of Teachers of Mathematics. NCTM Yearbook.

Davidson, N. & Gulick F. (1976). *Abstract algebra: An active learning approach.* Boston, MA: Houghton Mifflin.

Davidson, N. & Kroll, D. L. (1991). An overview of research on cooperative learning related to mathematics. *Journal for Research in Mathematics Education, 22*(5), 362-365.

Davidson, N., McKeen, R. & Eisenberg, T. (1973). Curriculum construction with student input. *The Mathematics Teacher*, March, 271-275.

Deutsch, M. (1960). The effects of cooperation and competition upon group process. In D. Cartwright & A. Zander (Eds.), *Group dynamics: Research and theory* (2nd Ed.). New York, NY: Harper & Row.

Dewey, J. (1916). *Democracy and education.* New York, NY: Macmillan. (Republished by Collier, 1966).

Dewey, J. (1938). *Experience and education.* New York, NY: Kappa Delta Pi. (Republished by Collier, 1966).

Hagelgans, N., Reynolds, B., et al. (1995). *Practical guide to cooperative learning in collegiate mathematics.* Mathematical Association of America. MAA Notes Series #37.

Leikin, R. & Zaslavsky, O. (1999). Cooperative learning in mathematics. *The Mathematics Teacher, 92*(3), 240-246.

McKeen, R. & Davidson, N. (1975). An alternative to individual instruction in mathematics. *American Mathematical Monthly*, December, 1006-1009.

Moise, E.E. (1965). Activity and motivation in mathematics. *American Mathematical Monthly, 72*(4), 407-412.

Rogers, B., Reynolds, B., Davidson, N., &Thomas, A. (2002). *Cooperative learning in undergraduate mathematics: Issues that matter and strategies that work.* Mathematical Association of America. MAA Notes Series #55.

University of Maryland Mathematics Project. (Cole, M., Davidson, N., Fey, J., Henkelman, J., et al.). (1978). *Unifying concepts and processes in elementary mathematics.* Boston, MA: Allyn & Bacon.

Urion D. & Davidson, N. (1992). Student achievement in small-group instruction versus teacher-centered instruction. *Primus, 2*(3), 257-264.

Weissglass, J. (1976). Small groups: An alternative to the lecture method. *The Two-Year College Mathematics Journal, 7*, 15-20.

White, R. &Lippitt, R. (1960). Leader behavior and member reaction in three "social climates." In D. Cartwright & A. Zander (Eds.), *Group dynamics: Research and theory* (2nd Ed.). New York, NY: Harper & Row.

Neil Davidson. University of Maryland, Professor Emeritus
  With editorial input from:
Barbara J. Millis, former Director of four faculty development centers (retired)
Richard D. Solomon. University of Maryland (retired)

Personal Retrospective on a Lengthy Career with the Scholarship of Teaching and Learning (SoTL)

I did not plan to have a 50-year career with the scholarship of teaching and learning (SoTL); it just developed over time. In fact, the term SoTL did not exist when I began my work with cooperative learning in the mid 1960s. Back then we simply called it research on teaching

That work began with my dissertation on developing the small group discovery method of mathematics instruction (Davidson 1970, 1971), later known as a form of cooperative learning. An overview of the genesis of that work, based on the scholarships of integration and application, is presented in another essay in this volume. It includes a number of publications on research, theoretical comparisons, curriculum development, and classroom practice in mathematics teaching.

As a professor emeritus, I am still active in scholarly writing, presentations, and teaching short courses. In the first 25 years or so of my career, I focused on teaching and learning in mathematics; in the later years, I expanded this to included teaching and learning in general. This article will focus on personal anecdotes about various projects and publications over the years that I hope will prove useful to younger colleagues seeking to build careers in teaching and learning.

This essay on SoTL is divided into six sections: cooperative learning, public presentations, doctoral programs and dissertations, teacher education and staff development, university faculty development, and reflections and recommendations.

Cooperative Learning

In 1979, Shlomo Sharan, after hearing of my work in small group learning in math, invited me to participate in the first international convention on cooperation in education, held in Israel. Some participants were surprised to learn that small groups could be used in mathematics since, in their view, there was nothing to discuss in math. At the convention, people who had been instrumental in developing small group approaches for learning met one another for the first time, and some of us became long-term colleagues and friends. I was fortunate to be in the right place at the right time with the right people.

At the convention, we formed a new professional association, the International Association for the Study of Cooperation in Education (IASCE). It fostered development of theory, research, curriculum, and classroom practice in cooperation in education.

It offered some published books, a Newsletter, and periodic international conferences. The first major book published by the IASCE included two of my papers (Davidson, 1980 a, b), the first on introducing small group learning in mathematics to non-mathematicians, and the second on using Re-evalution Counseling to change education. Later conferences of the IASCE led to a paper reviewing CL research in math (Davidson, 1985) and one by Robertson, Davidson, and Dees (1999) in the Handbook by S. Sharan.

For me, the IASCE is a wonderful source of stimulation, new learning, keeping up with the field, and collegial support. (I became its fourth President in 1990, following Richard Schmuck, Shlomo Sharan, and Robert Slavin.) In addition to these leaders, I also got to work with other early major contributors and many more in later years. If this paper were not a personal retrospective, I would be citing works by these eminent scholars.

Reflections: Conferences are valuable because of the people you interact with and the opportunities to present your work (a SoTL premise). When you offer presentations/workshops at conferences, you receive feedback from colleagues/peers and from workshop participants. This feedback leads to reflection (SoTL) and subsequent actions/changes. Conference presentations can also lead to publications, and vice-versa.

In the IASCE conference in 1985, we founded three regional associations to support teachers with staff development for cooperative learning. Bob Slavin and I proposed the Mid-Atlantic Association for Cooperation in Education (MAACIE), which Frank Lyman and I led for many years. Our active, cross-functional board consisted of faculty, teachers, staff developers, and principals. MAACIE published a newsletter and offered a variety of CL workshops for thousand of teachers, as did its sister organizations CACIE and GLACIE. MAACIE organized and hosted the 1990 international conference of the IASCE. MAACIE received an award for excellence in staff development from the Maryland Council of Staff Developers.

Reflections: An international organization focused on theory and research can lead to the formation of regional associations focused on practical implementation, teaching, and staff development. This can change the teaching styles of thousands of teachers and can lead to further reflective practice by these educators.

At an IASCE conference in 1985, Mark Brubacher and colleagues were talking about collaborative learning, which was new to me. They edited a book with broad perspectives including both cooperative and collaborative learning (Brubacher et al, 1990). The book included a chapter on applying Perry's cognitive development scheme to small group cooperative learning (Davidson and Shearn, 1990).

For many years, a puzzling theoretical issue in the field was the relationship between cooperative and collaborative learning. A set of publications addressed this question (Brubacher et al, 1990; Davidson 1994, 2002; Mathews, Cooper, Davidson, & Hawkes, 1995). This culminated in a volume describing and analyzing four forms of small group learning: cooperative, collaborative, problem-based, and team-based learning (Davidson, Major, & Michaelsen, 2014). (This volume, based on the scholarship of integration, is summarized in a separate essay in this book.)

The volume on approaches to small group learning arose also from the stimulation of the Lilly Conferences on College Teaching, where all four of these approaches were presented separately. For thirty-five years, teacher-scholars from across the U.S. and internationally have gathered annually to share innovative pedagogies and discuss insights about teaching and learning at the Lilly Conference in Ohio, and several others around the USA.

Reflections: By pursuing a puzzling line of inquiry over many years, and sharing results in conferences and papers, scholars might be enabled to present an integrative synthesis which encompasses different perspectives.

Working with co-authors or co-editors enables one to incorporate different approaches, to provide constructive feedback to one another, and to produce works which are better than the authors could accomplish individually.

At an IASCE conference in the 1990s, some of us were talking about the need for professional development for cooperative learning; most faculty cannot learn these techniques simply by reading. We found that approaches to faculty development for CL varied considerably. Celeste Brody and I decided to create an edited volume on this theme, including multiple viewpoints on professional development for CL. The result was the book by Brody and Davidson (1998).

In the late 1980s I became interested in the connection between higher order thinking skills (HOTS) and cooperative learning. An acronym suddenly popped into mind: HOTSICLE. That stands for Higher Order Thinking Skills in Cooperative Learning Environments. I immediately conceived the idea of a book on this topic, and formed a partnership with Toni Worsham, an expert on thinking studies. The result was an edited book on enhancing thinking through cooperative learning (Davidson & Worsham, 1992). It brought together multiple perspectives on thinking and learning, and was far beyond the capabilities of any single author.

Reflections: Edited books can be a legitimate form of SoTL, especially when they are comprehensive, include multiple perspectives, and provide integrative syntheses.

Perhaps because of this book, I was invited by the Regional Training Center (RTC) to design a graduate course for teachers in three states, dealing with enhancing thinking through cooperative learning. My teacher education partner Richard Solomon and I designed the course, created a handbook for participants and an instructors' manual, and trained a cadre of instructors to teach the course. The first edition of the course used a framework of teaching for, of, and about thinking. The second edition is entitled "Encouraging skillful, critical, and creative thinking." The handbook is by Solomon and Davidson (2009) and the instructors' manual by Davidson and Solomon (2009).

Kathleen Carroll and I developed a graduate course and handbook on classroom assessment techniques for teachers, also through the RTC. The second edition of the course, which employed cooperative learning throughout, was entitled "Assessment techniques." (Carroll and Davidson, 2009).

Another handbook dealt with relationship activities for cooperative and collegial learning (Solomon, Davidson, and Solomon, 1993). Related papers on varied topics were published by Solomon and Davidson (1990, 1992, 1993, 1996, 2009).

Doing a long-term project such as a book or new curriculum can be tiring and discouraging. In my case, a passionate commitment to the topic helped me carry it through to completion.

Every project mentioned so far was conducted on a zero budget with no external funding.

Reflections: Careful development of a textbook can be a legitimate aspect of SoTL, especially when the book is field-tested with one's own students, refined and polished through observation and feedback. If colleagues also use the book, they can provide constructive critique and suggestions for improvement.

Funding is desirable and sometimes essential, but there are plenty of worthwhile studies that can be done on a shoestring without funding.

For a long-term SoTL project, a passionate commitment to the topic area is needed to carry it through to completion.

Public Presentations

One aspect of SoTL is public presentation of one's work. I have had the opportunity to give hundreds of presentations ranging from keynote addresses and plenary sessions to research papers to workshops for teachers. Venues ranged from professional conferences to college and universities to school districts.

For example, in the 1990s, I was invited to offer multiple faculty development workshops through the centers for learning and teaching and academic departments in each of these settings: Arizona State University, the University of Michigan, Grand Valley State University, and of course the University of Maryland.

Among my dozens of presentations at Lilly Conferences, a recent one deals with helping introverts to thrive in structured cooperative groups -- unlike the unstructured group work where they can be intimidated by fast talkers and dominators (Davidson, 2015). This is the first theoretical work establishing that connection.

Another recent presentation is a full-day preconference on cooperative and collaborative learning (Davidson and Millis, 2015 and 2016). The presentation involves theory and research on cooperative learning, theoretical distinctions between approaches, a variety of practical techniques, active engagement in learning, reflection on experience, and the connection between cooperative learning and deep learning.

Reflections: Presentations at conferences or educational institutions are valuable because of the people you interact with and the opportunities to present your work (a SoTL premise). When you offer presentations/workshops at conferences, you receive feedback from colleagues/peers and from workshop participants. This feedback leads to reflection (SoTL) and subsequent actions/changes. Conference presentations can also lead to publications, and vice-versa.

In presenting my first 75 or so cooperative learning workshops for faculty, I almost always encountered a point of resistance. Participants balked when hearing the research that cooperative learning is superior to lectures in promoting student achievement. Viewing that research as a "putdown" of the lecture method, they argued in defense of lecturing.

In a hilarious conversation about this resistance, Emily Jensen and I created a "twelve step recovery program for lectureholics (professors addicted to lecturing)." The key idea of our program, which is based on the life-changing Alcoholics Anonymous steps, is to respect the importance of lecturing but to get it under control by alternating brief lectures (lecturettes) with short pair or group activities (groupettes). That approach keeps students awake and engaged. We have presented this program about a hundred times with high levels of participant satisfaction and no resistance (Jensen and Davidson, 1997).

Reflections: Analyzing the flaws and sticky points in one's presentation can lead to a new version that is more satisfactory.

It is best to reflect soon after the presentation and write down what went well and what needs improvement.

It helps to remain open to faculty concerns, keep a sense of humor, and present new ideas with humor, freshness, and a lack of defensiveness.

Doctoral Programs and Dissertations

Graduate teaching includes mentoring the next generation of scholars by fostering and advising doctoral students' research. In leading the doctoral research proposal seminar for many years, we learned to balance challenge and support: setting high standards and supporting students to meet them. The structure for this included students reading and critiquing each other's research proposals, which were exchanged by email. To set a constructive tone of supporting the person while critiquing the document to improve it, students and faculty followed these steps in the critique session: (1) positive aspects of this proposal, (2) questions for clarification, and (3) suggestions for improvement. Applying this structure, I served as major advisor (or co-advisor in a few cases) for 75 doctoral graduates.

At one point in serving on doctoral committees, I became frustrated by some doctoral students doing insubstantial studies via technically correct experimental designs. In response, I wrote a humorous satirical essay outlining a 22-step process that a high school student could use to write a doctoral dissertation with a simplistic experimental design. That essay was a blend of fantasy and reality. Apparently, it contained enough structure and practical suggestions to help students to design and carry out their studies – hopefully substantial ones. I was invited many times to present the satire in seminars on designing the doctoral research proposal. The essay has not yet been published. (I don't know where to send it.)

Colleagues Arends, Henkelman, Nash, and I offered a doctoral program in professional development based on learning communities and cohort groups. Each cohort group took all their courses together in a learning community emphasizing mutual support, active learning, reflection on experience, interpersonal and small group communication, organization development and culture, varied internship settings, and more. The doctoral completion rate for the first cohort group was over 60 percent, which was much higher than the 25 percent rate for the College of Education overall. However, we were disappointed by this result and aimed to increase it in the second cohort group. We hypothesized that the problem was this: intense community support during the coursework program was followed by isolated individual effort during the dissertation phase. We countered that by establishing a doctoral dissertation support group that met regularly to offer encouragement, sharing and presentations of work, and constructive peer critique. That intervention boosted the completion rate to 92 percent in the second cohort group (Henkelman and Davidson, 2014).

Reflections: A constructive process for peer feedback and editing of dissertation proposals improves their quality and likelihood of completion of the study.

Development of an entire doctoral program or improvement of an existing one are challenging SoTL ventures. They require thorough reflection on experience, gathering feedback from participants, observations of their work in class, assessing their learning through projects and papers, and holding community meetings with frank discussions of what is working well and what needs improvement. Attention to the feedback and making suitable program changes can lead to improved outcomes in terms of completion rate and can enhance the quality of dissertations.

Teacher Education and Staff Development

How can cooperative learning be incorporated into teacher education preparation programs? One research-based approach is a combination of theory, clear modeling, and practice opportunities with feedback. In applying this notion, we repeatedly demonstrate varied methods of cooperative learning in courses on methods of teaching. Students design lessons for CL, and practice by presenting short lessons to small groups of peers in videotaped microteaching sessions. Constructive feedback is provided by students and by the instructor. This is also done with other models of teaching such as the lecture, concept attainment model, and behavioral skill mastery model (Arends, 1998; Lyman and Davidson, 2004).

In addition to my regular faculty role, I was invited by Jim Greenberg and Maurice Erly to serve as coordinator of an innovative student teaching program through the Office of Laboratory Experiences, and did so for 17 years. Several middle and senior high schools with innovative principals in Prince George's County, MD, became professional development centers for the preparation of student teachers. Each school had a small, interdisciplinary school-based supervision team of outstanding teachers who took responsibility for the student teaching program at their school. They learned to function as field-based teacher educators and staff developers with unusually high levels of professional responsibility. My co-coordinator Richard Solomon and I offered a series of graduate courses, providing intensive staff development for the teams. This program won an award for excellence in staff development from the Maryland Council of Staff Developers. Professional conference presentations about the program sometimes included several of our supervising teachers. One example of this was by Solomon, Davidson et al (1990).

The Clinical Classroom Project, developed by Arends and Murphy, brought together teacher educators from colleges and universities. We who participated functioned as demonstration teachers, opened up our classrooms to observers and conferred with them about the lessons. We also gave demonstration lessons to provide modeling of active learning techniques for teachers in their own classrooms with their own students (Winitzky and Arends, 1991). In debriefing sessions after the lessons, observers and I learned by analyzing what I did and why, what went well, and how the lesson could be improved

I had the opportunity to participate in two major workshops with Madeline Hunter, founder of the prominent seven-step Mastery Teaching model. Those stimulating workshops led me to see how to enhance her model by incorporating research-based cooperative learning practices in several of its phases (Davidson and O'Leary, 1990). This helped teachers who had been feeling confined to rigidly follow the steps of that model and who wanted a stronger research base for their teaching.

Reflections: Conducting SoTL projects in higher education has a parallel in conducting research on teaching in schools. In fact, the long tradition of research on teaching in schools pre-dates the notion of SoTL in higher education.

Teachers at all levels can learn to do reflective practice and conduct inquiries about their own classroom teaching.

Teachers can improve their use of varied models of teaching by presenting short lessons to small groups of peers in videotaped microteaching sessions, with constructive critique afterward.

University Faculty Development

For several years at the University of Maryland, I worked closely with Jim Greenberg in the Center for Teaching Excellence, providing workshops for faculty, department consultations on teaching, and developing a faculty consultation program for individual faculty who wanted to improve their teaching. One outgrowth of my work with CTE was a publication reflecting on practical implementation of small group learning (Davidson, 1998), which was an example of the scholarship of application.

For three years, I co-led with Greenberg the Lilly Fellows program – a faculty learning community group of ten faculty members who met regularly to talk about teaching and learning. Each group developed it own project. In one year, I proposed creating an Academy of Excellence in Teaching and Learning (AETL). This would expand the yearly Lilly Fellows program into an ongoing community of faculty who have shown outstanding devotion to teaching and learning and who strive to enhance its quality and status in this research university. The project proposal was written by Alt, Assad, Davidson, and Varner (1999). That project succeeded in establishing the AETL, which still continues. One of its goals is to stimulate faculty participation in SoTL.

My work in the Center for Teaching Excellence (CTE) led to an appointment as Associate Dean for Undergraduate Studies with Dean Robert Hampton. My responsibilities included continuing work with CTE and promotion of SoTL campus-wide, partly through participation in the academies of the Carnegie Foundation for the Advancement of Teaching. We found that some departments were receptive to SoTL publications and others, unfortunately, would not accept them for promotion and tenure.

Reflections: A faculty learning community can provide a vibrant source of support for teaching and learning and for SoTL.

Campus-wide leadership is need to encourage and legitimize faculty participation in SoTL for promotion and tenure.

Before embarking on a career in SoTL, faculty should check whether that is valued for tenure and promotion at their institution. If not, they would need to decide whether to take the risk of becoming a test case and perhaps a change agent for SoTL on their campus.

Personal reflections: It is paradoxical that with a doctorate in mathematics, I am not attracted to doing empirical studies with statistical analysis, and have only done a few of them. (I admire those who do that work consistently and productively.) My publications mainly include theoretical works, integrative synthesis papers, comparison and contrast pieces, qualitative inquiry, descriptions of new ideas, practical "how to do it" papers, training manuals, program development, and curriculum development. All these, if carried out in a scholarly and reflective fashion, can be examples of SoTL.

It has been my good fortune to work with innovative, creative, and congenial colleagues. But several times, in racing ahead to develop a major project with a tight deadline, we did not build in a research component. This was a missed opportunity for SoTL inquiry.

Reflections and Recommendations

Although this is my personal retrospective, it might have implications for faculty interested in intensive work with SoTL. I would have benefitted from knowing some of these ideas earlier in my career. Here are some reflections and recommendations.

Remember that work on the scholarship of teaching and learning is a worthwhile professional endeavor. Teaching and learning should be the major raison d'etre for any college or university.

SoTL projects can develop through reflection, analysis, and research on your own classroom teaching. Your teaching and research are intertwined.

Before embarking on a career in SoTL, check whether that is valued for tenure and promotion at your institution. If not, you would need to decide whether to take the risk of becoming a test case and perhaps a change agent for SoTL on your campus.

Campus-wide leadership is need to encourage and legitimize faculty participation in SoTL for promotion and tenure.

For the long run, pick an area of inquiry in SoTL about which you are passionate and care deeply.

Use approaches to inquiry that are compatible with your own personal style and preferences. Some scholars are "quants" while others are "quals" and others are theoreticians (synthesizers or integrators), philosophers, historians, curriculum developers, practical appliers, or program evaluators. The style and standards for scholarly excellence will vary among the categories.

If you are an abstract conceptualizer, you might be able to conceive of an entire multi-year program of research. Yet most of us are content to think ahead with one or two projects in mind.

Keep a journal or logbook wherein you record your ideas for SoTL inquiry when they pop into mind. "Absent minded professors" might generate many ideas but forget them, having not written them down.

Conferences are valuable because of the people you interact with and the opportunities to present your work (a SoTL premise). When you offer presentations/workshops at conferences, you receive feedback from colleagues/peers and from workshop participants. This feedback leads to reflection (SoTL) and subsequent actions and changes. Conference presentations can also lead to publications, and vice-versa.

A faculty learning community can provide a vibrant source of support for teaching and learning and for SoTL.

If you are socially motivated, look for people and projects for collaborative effort. Find at least one partner with whom you have synergy for research, writing, project development, or presentations.

Form research teams of compatible people with different styles of inquiry to create a richer, more comprehensive investigation.

Remember the power of personal connections, where colleagues become mutually supportive friends. Before submitting a paper for publication, ask some friendly colleagues for a constructive critique of it.

A constructive process for peer feedback and editing of dissertation proposals improves their quality and likelihood of completion of the study.

Learn from other people as well as from the literature. Be thankful for the teachers and colleagues who have positively influenced your education and career.

Participate in professional conferences of interest to you and give talks when possible. Recognize that publications can lead to presentations, since you have something to say, and vice versa.

Analyzing the flaws and sticky points in one's presentation can lead to a new version that is more satisfactory. It is best to reflect soon after the presentation and write down what went well and what needs improvement. It helps to remain open to faculty concerns, keep a sense of humor, and present new ideas with humor, freshness, and a lack of defensiveness.

Funding is desirable and sometimes essential, but know that there are plenty of worthwhile studies that can be done on a shoestring without funding.

If writing a book seems too daunting, you can write a series of related papers, one at a time, and later incorporate them into one volume.

An edited book can be a legitimate form of SoTL, especially when it is comprehensive, brings together multiple perspectives, and provides integrative syntheses. This can be far beyond the capabilities of any single author.

A carefully developed major textbook or curriculum development effort can be a SoTL contribution , especially when it is field-tested with one's own students, and refined and polished through observation and feedback. If colleagues also use the book, they can provide constructive critique and suggestions for improvement.

Conducting SoTL projects in higher education has a parallel in conducting research on teaching in schools. In fact, the long tradition of research on teaching in schools predates the notion of SoTL in higher education. School/university collaborative projects can offer a fertile source of SoTL inquiry.

Development and refinement of an entire program or improvement of an existing one are challenging SoTL ventures. They require thorough reflection on experience and employing varied methods for SoTL inquiry. Before embarking on a major innovative project, make sure to build in a research component right from the start.

Teachers at all levels can learn to do reflective practice and conduct inquiries about their own classroom teaching.

Teachers can improve their use of varied models of teaching by presenting short lessons to small groups of peers in videotaped microteaching sessions, with constructive critique afterward.

More senior and established faculty receive more invitations for boards of directors, review panels, speaking engagements, and publications. Success builds on success. Faculty can grow in this regard over time.

References

Arends, R. (1998). *Learning to teach*. Boston, MA: McGraw Hill.

Asch, S.E. (1960). Effects of group pressure upon the modification and distortion of judgments. In D. Cartwright & A. Zander (Eds.), *Group dynamics: Research and theory* (2nd Ed.). New York, NY: Harper & Row.

Bales, R. F. & Borgatta, E. F. (1961). Size of group as a factor in the interaction profile. In A. P. Hare, E.

F. Borgatta, & R. F. Bales. *Small groups, studies in social interaction.* New York, NY: Alfred A. Knopf.

Brody, C. & Davidson, N. (Eds). (1998). *Professional development for cooperative learning: Issues and approaches.* Albany, NY: SUNY Press.

Cartwright, D. & Zander, A. (1960). *Group dynamics: Research and theory* (2nd ed.). New York, NY: Harper & Row.

Dancis, J. & Davidson, N. (1970). The Texas method and the small group discovery method. In *The Legacy of R. L. Moore.* (online and on CD)

Davidson, N. (1970, 1971a). *The small discovery method of mathematics instruction as applied in calculus.* Doctoral dissertation: University of Wisconsin, Madison. Published in 1971 by the Wisconsin Research and Development Center for Cognitive Learning.

Davidson, N. (1971b). The small group discovery method as applied in calculus instruction. *American Mathematical Monthly.* August-September, 789-791.

Davidson, N. (1976). Motivation of students in small-group learning of mathematics. *Frostburg State College Journal of Mathematics Education, 11,* 1-18.

Davidson, N. (1979. The small-group discovery method: 1976-77. In Harvey, J. & Romberg, T. (Eds.). *Problem solving studies in mathematics.* Madison, WI: The Wisconsin Research and Development Center for Individualized Schooling.

Davidson, N. (1980). Small-group learning and teaching in mathematics: An introduction for non-mathematicians. In Sharan, S., Hare, P., Webb, C., & Hertz-Lazarowitz, R. (Eds.). *Cooperation in education* (pp. 136-145). Provo, UT: Brigham Young University Press.

Davidson, N. (1980). Using reevaluation counseling to change education. In Sharan, S., Hare, P., Webb, C., & Hertz-Lazarowitz, R. (Eds.). *Cooperation in education* (pp.182-194). Provo, UT: Brigham Young University Press.

Davidson, N. (1985). Small-group learning in mathematics: A selective review of the research. In Slavin, R., et al. (Eds.). *Learning to cooperate, cooperating to learn.* New York, NY: Plenum Press.

Davidson, N. (Ed.) (1990). *Cooperative learning in mathematics: A handbook for teachers.* Menlo Park, CA: Addison-Wesley (available through Dale Seymour).

Davidson, N. (1990). Small group cooperative learning in mathematics. In T. Cooney (Ed.). *Teaching and learning mathematics in the 1990s.* Reston, VA: National Council of Teachers of Mathematics. NCTM Yearbook.

Davidson, N. (1994, second edition 2002). Cooperative and collaborative learning: An integrative perspective. In J. Thousand, R. Villa, & A. Nevin (Eds.). *Creativity and collaborative learning: A practical guide for empowering teachers and students* (pp. 13-30). Baltimore, MD: Brookes Publishing.

Davidson, N. (1998). Small-group cooperative learning: What I have learned in the past thirty years. In S. Selden, et al. (Eds.). *Essays on quality learning* (pp. 169-178). University of Maryland. IBM Total Quality Project.

Davidson, N. (2015). *How to help introverts thrive in cooperative groups.* Presentation at the International Lilly Conference on College Teaching. Miami University, Ohio.

Davidson, N. & Gulick F. (1976). *Abstract algebra: An active learning approach.* Boston, MA: Houghton Mifflin.

Davidson, N. & Kroll, D.L. (1991). An overview of research on cooperative learning related to mathematics. *Journal for Research in Mathematics Education, 22*(5), 362-365.

Davidson, N. and Shearn, E. (1990). Use of small group teaching and cognitive developmental instruction in a mathematical course for prospective elementary school teachers. In M. Brubacher, R. Payne, & K. Rickett (Eds.), *Perspectives on small group learning: Theory and practice* (pp. 309-327). Canada: Rubicon.

Davidson, N., McKeen, R. & Eisenberg, T. (1973). Curriculum construction with student input. *The Mathematics Teacher*, March, 271-275.

Davidson, N., Agreen, L., & Davis, C. (1978). Small group learning in junior high school mathematics. *School Science and Mathematics, 1*, 23-20.

Davidson, N. & Worsham, T. (1992). *Enhancing thinking through cooperative learning.* New York, NY: Teachers College Press.

Davidson, N. & O'Leary, P. (1990). How cooperative learning can enhance mastery teaching. *Educational Leadership.* February, 30-34

Davidson, N., Major, C., & Michaelsen, L. (Eds). (2014). Small group learning in higher education – Cooperative, collaborative, problem-based and team-based learning. *Journal on Excellence in College Teaching, 25*(3&4).

Deutsch, M. (1960). The effects of cooperation and competition upon group process. In D. Cartwright & A. Zander (Eds.), *Group dynamics: Research and theory* (2nd Ed.). New York, NY: Harper & Row.

Dewey, J. (1916). *Democracy and education.* New York, NY: Macmillan. (Republished by Collier, 1966).

Dewey, J. (1938). *Experience and education.* New York: Kappa Delta Pi. (Republished by Collier, 1966).

Hagelgans, N., Reynolds, B., et al. (1995). *Practical guide to cooperative learning in collegiate mathematics.* Mathematical Association of America. MAA Notes Series #37.

Henkelman, J. & Davidson, N. (2014). Building a learning community in a doctoral programme in professional development. In B. Cocklin, K. Coombe, & J. Retallick (Eds.), *Learning communities in education* (pp. 230-246). London, England: Routledge.

Lyman, F. & Davidson, N. (2004). Cooperative learning in preservice teacher education at the University of Maryland. In Cohen, E., Brody, C., and Sapon-Shevin, M. *Teaching cooperative learning: The challenge for teacher education* (pp. 83-95). Albany: State University of New York Press.

Matthews, R. S., Cooper, J. L., Davidson, N., & and Hawkes, P. (1995). Building bridges between cooperative and collaborative learning. *Change, 27*(4), 34-37.

McKeen, R. & Davidson, N. (1975). An alternative to individual instruction in mathematics. *American Mathematical Monkthly, 82*(10), 1006-1009.

Moise, E.E. (1965). Activity and motivation in mathematics. *American Mathematical Monthly, 72*(4), 407-412.

Robertson, L., Davidson, N., & Dees, R. (1999). Cooperative learning to support thinking, reasoning, and communicating in mathematics. In Sharan, S. (Ed,). *Handbook of cooperative learning methods.* Westport, CT: Greenwood.

Rogers, B., Reynolds, B., Davidson, N., & Thomas, A. (2002). *Cooperative learning in undergraduate mathematics: Issues that matter and strategies that work.* Mathematical Association of America. MAA Notes Series #55.

Solomon, R. D., & Davidson, N. (1990). *Collaborating with schools from a campus-based perspective.* Presentation at the American Association for Higher Education Conference on School/College Collaboration. Chicago, IL. 6/19/90.

Solomon, R., & Davidson, N. (1990). Cooperative learning and the relationship skills: Tools for positive social development. Co*operative Learning*, *11*(2), 25-27.

Solomon, R., Davidson, N., & Solomon, E. (1992). Some thinking skills and social skills that facilitate cooperative learning. In N. Davidson & T. Worsham (Eds.), *Enhancing thinking through cooperative learning* (pp. 101-119). New York, NY: Teacher's College Press.

Solomon, R. & Davidson, N. (1993). Cooperative dimensions of learning. *Cooperative Learning, 13*(2), 37-43.

Solomon, R. & Davidson, N. (1996). Staff development in cooperative learning using cooperative structures and relationship skills. In H, Rimmerman (Ed.), *Resources in cooperative learning.* San Juan Capistrano, CA: Kagan Cooperative Learning.

Solomon, R, & Davidson, N. (2009). Cooperative learning: Research and implementation for Jewish education. *Jewish Educational Leadership, 7*(3).

Solomon, R. D., & Davidson, N. (2009). Encouraging skillful, critical, and creative thinking. *Graduate course handbook.* Randolph, NJ: Regional Training Center.

Solomon, R., Davidson, N., & Solomon, E. (1993). *The handbook for the fourth r: Relationship activities for cooperative and collegial learning, Vol. III.* Columbia, MD: National Institute for Relationship Training.

University of Maryland Mathematics Project. (Cole, M., Davidson, N., Fey, J., & Henkelman, J.). (1978). *Unifying concepts and processes in elementary mathematics.* Boston: Allyn and Bacon.

Urion, D. & Davidson, N. (1992). Student achievement in small-group instruction versus teacher-centered instruction. *Primus, 2*(3), 257-264.

Weissglass, J. (1976). Small groups: An alternative to the lecture method. *The Two-Year College Mathematics Journal. 7,* 15-20.

White, R. & Lippitt, R. (1960). Leader behavior and member reaction in three "social climates." In D. Cartwright & A. Zander (Eds.), *Group dynamics: Research and theory* (2nd Ed.). New York, NY: Harper & Row.

Winitzki, N. & Arends, R. (1991). Translating research into practice: The effects of various forms of training and clinical experience on preservice students' knowledge, skill, and reflectiveness. *Journal of Teacher Education, 42*(1), 52-65

Neil Davidson, University of Maryland, Professor Emeritus
    With editorial input from
Barbara J. Millis, former Director of four faculty development centers (retired)
Richard D. Solomon. University of Maryland (retired)

Part B. Theoretical Perspectives

The Theoretical Framework: Gatekeeper to the Scholarship of Teaching & Learning

Background

Under the umbrella of the Scholarship of Teaching and Learning (SoTL), most teacher-researchers examine the effects of a teaching experiment, intending to produce new or different learning in their classrooms. Fundamentally, this is known as "action research," relating a hypothesis about a teaching action on a learning outcome (Torrence & Pryor, 2001). And, although SoTL certainly invokes action research, a critical component to the process is moving from theorizing to testing and back to theorizing. In essence, to merit the construct of scholarship, the work must consider the challenging-yet-fruitful question: "Why did(n't) this work?"

The Gate *into* SoTL

Within an educational study, a theoretical framework is used "to explain, predict, and understand phenomena, and in many cases, to challenge and extend existing knowledge" (Swanson & Chermack, 2013). Without it, action research is merely story-telling. Unfortunately, for faculty members outside the social sciences, the application of learning theories to pedagogy will likely be unknown territory (Frodeman, 2010). Furthermore, even those familiar with conducting educational research may need assistance distinguishing between a *review of literature* (a critical and evaluative synthesis of writings related to a topic) and a *theoretical framework* (a systemic explanation used to make sense of data).

Helping Faculty to Build and Write a Theoretical Framework

As part of a mid-career professional learning community, a subset of six faculty from a diverse set of disciplines (including chemistry, mathematics, religion, and theatre) formed a team of "critical friends" dedicated to planning, implementing, and writing on a SoTL experiment within each of their respective classrooms. At the end of the first meeting of the semester-long PLC, the team recognized a need to explicitly devote time and deed toward the building of a theoretical framework supporting the studies. As a result, the following three-week plan was developed to assist faculty through the theoretical gate:

Week One: Finding a Foundation (60 minute session)

- As a group, discuss the meaning and purpose of a theoretical foundation. (20 minutes)
- Individually, search for an educational theory that might be useful in describing potential results for your teaching experiment, starting at the Learning Theory Mapping Site (http://cmapspublic3.ihmc.us/rid=1LGVGJY66-CCD-5CZ-12G3/Learning%20The). (30 minutes)
- With a partner, relay how the theory(ies) you have explored may connect with the hypothesis you are proposing. (10 minutes)

Inter-Session Work

Conduct more research on educational theories, finding at least three pillars or founding tenets that support a reason for conducting your teaching experiment. Note: these pillars may come from different theories.

Week Two: The Writing Circle (75 minute session)

- With your partner, provide a quick "check-in" to recount findings from the inter-session work. (10 minutes)
- Individually, write three questions (each on a separate index card), concerning

how your partner's experiment connects with the proposed pillars. Do not share immediately; the questions will be referenced later in the session. (5 minutes)
- Individually, write what you have learned about educational theory(ies), attempting to connect the pillars to your teaching experiment. (40 minutes)
- With your partner, exchange and read writings. If your questions were answered, cross-reference the ideas on the index card and the writing itself. Return the writing (along with your index cards) to the author. (20 minutes)

Inter-Session Work

Prepare a "more-polished" draft of your writing of a theoretical framework. If warranted, address any unanswered questions posed by your partner.

Week Three: Sharing Frameworks (60 minute session)

- With your partner, discuss latest drafts, including how you addressed any of the unanswered questions (or why they remain unanswered). (10 minutes)
- As a group, share the basic outline of your theoretical framework, highlighting the connections between educational theories and your hypothesis. (5 minutes each, with transitions a total of 40 minutes)
- Individually, do a post-presentation write-up that (a) offers ideas/comments/suggestions to others and share the writing as may be appropriate, and/or (b) sketches how the work done by other members may be incorporated into your own framework. (10 minutes)

The Gate *Out of* SoTL

Although a critical component to SoTL, a theoretical framework should not obstruct a faculty member from beginning action research. The intent of the three week session was not to "finish the theory-portion of a report." Rather, it was to help gain entree into doing the research and (perhaps, more importantly) to provide a hook necessitating the explanation for why something did (not) work when analyzing data (see figure below).

How a Theoretical Framework Acts as a Gatekeeper

Furthermore, after an analysis of the work, faculty should return to the framework to determine whether or not educational theories can be extended. In doing so, the hope is to help others understand the interplay between teaching and learning, making practice public and moving from hypothesis (a specific conjecture for a particular situation) to theory (prediction of events in a broad, general context). As such, the work transcends disciplinary and pedagogical content knowledge, can be peer-reviewed, and completes the path to SoTL.

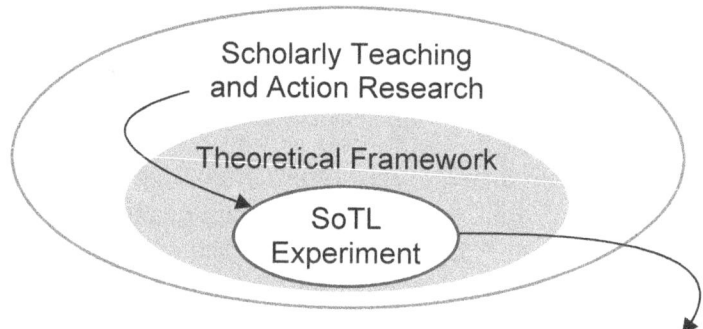

Reflections and Implications

Although team members were eager to "just get started" with their teaching experiments, the value of developing a theoretical framework became apparent over the course of the semester-long PLC. Faculty described the three-week plan as "an appropriate amount of time" to spend on theory and appreciated the structure used during the work sessions. Of note, the theoretical framework became an integral part of discussions when individuals began sharing progress reports on their teaching experiments. In fact, it was in the midst of collecting data that one of the members wrote in a journal, reflecting on the process of SoTL:

> I'm finding that my theoretical framework is causing me to adjust my questioning techniques in a class that I used to feel so comfortable in; I have a feeling that this is going to lead to another action research project entirely. Sigh. More questions than answers.

More questions, indeed.

References

Frodeman, R. (2010). *The Oxford handbook of interdisciplinarity*. Oxford University Press.

Swanson, R. A., & Chermack, T. J. (2013). *Theory building in applied disciplines*. Berrett-Koehler Publishers.

Torrance, H., & Pryor, J. (2001). Developing formative assessment in the classroom: Using action research to explore and modify theory. *British Educational Research Journal, 27*(5), 615-631.

Jeffrey P. Smith, Otterbein University

Student-Faculty Collaboration in Higher Education

Students' first year of college, or graduate school, can be daunting and confusing if not downright overwhelming. Professors can play important roles in guiding students through this difficult time. However, in order to do so, we must challenge two commonly held attitudes that work against us: 1) Our desire to be maximally productive by just doing our research ourselves instead of involving students; and 2) Our perception that the student-mentor relationship occurs naturally, rather than because of our active outreach.

What Prevents Collaboration?

After being accepted into a competitive educational program, students may find themselves feeling lost or as if some sort of mistake has been made in the selection process. This situation is known as the "Imposter Phenomenon" (Cokley, McClain, Enciso & Martinez, 2013) and affects students from both the majority and minority cultures as well as both males and females (Castro, Jones, & Mirsalimi, 2004). However, some students are particularly at risk for feeling like imposters. The extent to which a student feels like an imposter is directly proportional to the student's perceived minority status stress. In other words, the degree to which students perceive themselves to be isolated, stereotyped, or experiencing microaggressions is directly correlated with believing that they "don't belong" in higher education. Academic mentors need to vigilantly confront these perceptions, even if they are unstated, and increase their outreach efforts to students who may be especially vulnerable to the imposter phenomenon.

Cokley, McClain, Enciso & Martinez (2013) also found that intersecting marginalization compounds the effects of imposter syndrome. For example, an LGBTQ+ Asian-American female is more likely to feel like an imposter than a heterosexual, cisgender Asian-American male. Although white males and females are equally vulnerable to feeling like imposters, minority female students are more at risk than minority male students (Castro, Jones, & Mirsalimi, 2004). The key to understanding this differential relationship is self-efficacy. Students are at higher risk for feeling like imposters when they believe that they are the cause of their failures but not their successes. To combat these views, educators need to actively create an environment that students perceive to be safe, fair, and nonjudgmental. Talking directly with students about the imposter phenomenon can be a helpful start.

What Facilitates Collaboration?

To facilitate meaningful collaboration with students, professors have two important tools at their disposal: supervision and relationships. Supervision refers to the fact that productivity is increased during observation. In other words, we are more likely to produce high quality work if someone is watching us, particularly our bosses, teachers, or mentors (Baumeister & Leary, 1995; McCarney, Warner, Iliffe, Van Haselen, Griffin & Fisher, 2007). This well-known "Hawthorne Effect" suggests that we should be actively involved in students' research instead of just allowing them to work independently and encouraging them to contact us "if they need help." This laissez faire method of research supervision is a prescription for failure, especially when combined with the aforementioned imposter phenomenon. Professors must also challenge our own notions about productivity. Although it may be quicker and easier in the long run to just churn out another article in our living room or lab, this more efficient choice does not benefit our students in the long run, for they must learn the valuable skills of researching a topic, designing an experiment, analyzing data, integrating ideas, and then writing a readable article.

Relationships are the second, and most valuable, tool we have for involving students in joint research projects. In fact, the importance of supervision pales in comparison to the importance of relationships, due to the fundamental human need to build interpersonal attachments (Baumeister & Leary, 1995). The need to relate to others is so strong that it is a primary motivator in our day-to-day behavior. Without significant attachments, individuals are prone to a host of negative outcomes, including impeded cognitive functioning and poor psychological well-being (Baumeister & Leary, 1995). A lack of significant relationships also increases the risk of students believing that they are imposters. Consider how vulnerable first-year students are to these risks as many of them are living away from home for perhaps the first time in their lives.

True collaborative relationships are the balm that cures these ills. In fact, a positive relationship between students and professors improves student productivity as well as academic performance (Decker, Dona, & Christenson, 2007; Toldson, Braithwaite, & Rentie, 2009). Students are more engaged, work harder, and produce more quality work when they perceive their professors care about them. To underscore this effect, Umbach & Wawrzynski (2005) found that students who reported more positive interactions with their professors were more likely to get involved in higher education endeavors such as research projects.

In conclusion, how can we promote collaboration between students and faculty?

1. Remember that a lack of approach does not imply a lack of interest. Instead, students may be reluctant to volunteer or get involved in projects because they are struggling with feelings of phoniness. Consistent efforts to reach out to students over time are thus paramount: one invitation to participate is rarely sufficient.
2. Students reflecting minority and/or traditionally marginalized backgrounds are particularly likely to need intentional, personal, and positive outreach efforts to participate in higher education projects. Students with intersecting ethnic, racial, sexual, gender, national, or religious identities that result in minority status stress are especially likely to feel the inherent power differential between professors and students.
3. As the Hawthorne Effect would imply, supervision is effective. Although, the student-mentor relationship is important, the research itself is often the purpose of the exercise, and thus productivity is very important. Students don't need to be micromanaged, but they do need our support, feedback, and guidance through the research process in order to produce high quality work. Thus, more frequent contact between students and faculty during larger research projects elevates the quality of the final project.

References

Baumeister, R. F., & Leary, M. R. (1995). The need to belong: desire for interpersonal attachments as a fundamental human motivation. *Psychological bulletin, 117*(3), 497.

Castro, D. M., Jones, R. A., & Mirsalimi, H. (2004). Parentification and the impostor phenomenon: An empirical investigation. *The American Journal of Family Therapy, 32*(3), 205-216.

Cokley, K., McClain, S., Enciso, A., & Martinez, M. (2013). An examination of the impact of minority status stress and impostor feelings on the mental health of diverse ethnic minority college students. *Journal of Multicultural Counseling and Development, 41*(2), 82-95

Decker, D. M., Dona, D. P., & Christenson, S. L. (2007). Behaviorally at-risk African American students:

The importance of student–teacher relationships for student outcomes. *Journal of School Psychology*, *45*(1), 83-109.

McCarney, R., Warner, J., Iliffe, S., Van Haselen, R., Griffin, M., & Fisher, P. (2007). The Hawthorne Effect: a randomized, controlled trial. *BMC medical research methodology*, *7*(1), 1.

Toldson, I. A., Braithwaite, R. L., & Rentie, R. J. (2009). Promoting college aspirations among school-age Black American males. Black American males in higher education: Research, programs and academe. *Diversity in Higher Education, 7,* 117-137.

Umbach, P. D., & Wawrzynski, M. R. (2005). Faculty do matter: The role of college faculty in student learning and engagement. *Research in Higher Education*, *46*(2), 153-184.

Truman Harris, Spalding University
Danniella Jones, Spalding University
DeDe Wohlfarth, Spalding University

The Fourth R, the Relationship Skills: Definition, Taxonomy, Procedures for Teaching, and Applications for Graduate Education

"Born into a family of Jewish immigrants, and living in multi-cultural environments in Bedford-Stuyvesant and Crown Heights, Brooklyn, New York, I quickly learned that in order to survive life in the neighborhood, I needed to acquire a set of skills that would empower me to get along with those who were different from me. Thus, the Fourth R, the relationship skills, emerged from my earliest experiences." (Richard D Solomon)

In this essay the authors will define and share the taxonomy and procedures for teaching the Fourth R, the relationship skills, to all learners, including graduate students and teachers.

The direct teaching of social skills to students is well documented in the literature (Cartledge & Milburn, 1978; Lynch & Simpson, 2010; Bremer & Smith, 2004). These studies have correlated social skills instruction with peer acceptance, improved student behavior, improved student-teacher relationships, and student achievement (American Psychological Association, 2015).

What is the Fourth R, the relationship skills?

Often termed "social skills" or "social-emotional skills," the Fourth R, the relationship skills, refers to the many intrapersonal, interpersonal, group and organizational social, emotional and cognitive competencies needed by both students and teachers. These relationship skills also empower students to manage their behavior so that they can individually and in groups achieve the learning objectives of the curriculum. But their impact goes beyond academics: Students need to get along with others in and outside of the classroom. These Fourth R skills also provide faculty or staff developers with the essential skills and activities to create a caring cooperative community of learners, to facilitate college or school-based change, and to mentor and supervise teachers. Moreover, the Fourth R provides teachers with the essential competencies to instruct the three R's of reading, writing, and arithmetic.

What is the taxonomy of the Fourth R?

Because the Fourth R construct is complex, its taxonomy is complex and comprehensive. Indeed, the Fourth R construct has four distinct levels.

The first level of the Fourth R is the intrapersonal dimension. On this first level learners, whether students or teachers, discover their internal ideas, emotions, experiences, preferences, values, biases, stereotypes, and inner messages.

The second level of the Fourth R is the interpersonal dimension. Learners retrieve their intrapersonal data and then face a cognitive challenge. Which of these intensely personal aspects of my inner self should I share with others and with whom? Putting these important decisions into action enables learners to master key relationship skills and competencies such as listening respectfully, asking open questions, paraphrasing, achieving consensus, and resolving interpersonal conflict.

On the third level of the Fourth R learners discover group relationship skills, including how to facilitate group discussions, how to play varied roles, and how to resolve group conflict.

Last, the fourth level of the Fourth R represents the organization relationship skills. On this dimension, learners discover more sophisticated tools that enable their ideas to be heard, discussed, modified, and ultimately embraced by larger groups of their peers. These complex relationship skills include, for example, knowing how to conduct a needs assessment, create an action plan, and develop a shared mission or vision statement in an organization.

The graphic below shows the specific relationship skills on each of the four levels of the Fourth R.

Graphic of the Four Levels of the Taxonomy of the Fourth R: The Relationship Skills

ORGANIZATIONAL RELATIONSHIP SKILLS (LEVEL IV)

TO REACH AGREEMENT ON A VISION, MISSION, THE GOAL(S), AND/OR OUTCOME(S) OF AN ORGANIZATION

▶ TO CONDUCT A NEEDS ASSESSMENT

TO CATEGORIZE, PRIORITIZE, AND SHARE DATA FROM THE NEEDS ASSESSMENT

GROUP RELATIONSHIP SKILLS (LEVEL III)

- IDENTIFY, DIAGNOSE, THE ROLES THAT PEOPLE PLAY IN GROUPS
- EVALUATE GROUP PERMORMANCE
- GROUP PROBLEM SOLVING

TO REACH AGREEMENT ON AN ANALYSIS OF THE PRIMARY PROBLEMS OF THE ORGANIZATION

INTERPERSONAL SKILLS (LEVEL II)

- SHARE ONE'S DATA, LISTEN TO THE DATA OF OTHERS
- APPLY FREE INFORMATION
- ASK OPEN QUESTIONS
- PARAPHRASE

- FISHBOWL FOR GROUP CONSENSUS
- ACHIEVE CONSENSUS
- PROBE
- CHECK FOR UNDER-STANDING

- RESOLVE CONFLICT

INTRAPERSONAL SKILLS (LEVEL I)

IDENTIFY ONE'S FACTS, CONCEPTS, PREFERENCES, INFORMED OPINIONS EXPERIENCES & FEELINGS, FIND FREE INFORMATION

- VALIDATE
- RESPECTFULLY LISTEN

- SURFACE HIDDEN AGENDA ITEMS OF GROUP
- HANDLE CRITICISM VIA THE BROKEN RECORD, NEGATIVE INQUIRY, & NEGATIVE ASSERTION
- SHOW ACCEPTANCE

- GIVE & RECEIVE TECHNICAL, POSITIVE, NEGATIVE & CORRECTIVE FEEDBACK
- JOIN & END A CONVERSATION

GROUP BRAIN-STORMING

MAKE GROUP DECISIONS

TO CREATE AN ACTION PLAN TO (A) ADDRESS THE PRIMARY PROBLEM(S), AND (B) ACHIEVE THE VISION, MISSION, GOAL(S) AND/OR OUTCOME(S) OF THE ORGANIZATION

- SHARE GROUP INFORMATION IN AN ORDERLY WAY
- ENVISION GROUP MISSION, GOALS, STANDARDS AND NORMS
- RESOLVE INTRA-GROUP CONFLICT VIA THE EIAG & TEAM MEETING

TO IMPLEMENT, MONITOR, AND EVALUATE THE ACTION PLAN

TO USE THE EVALUATION DATA FROM THE ACTION PLAN AS A NEW NEEDS ASSESSMENT TO EITHER (A) REVISE THE ACTION PLAN OR (B) RETHINK THE VISION, MISSION, GOAL(S), AND/OR OUTCOME(S)

Suggested Procedure for Teaching the Relationship Skills

Because of the complexity of the various levels, teachers must carefully select the appropriate Fourth R skills that correspond to the cognitive abilities of their students and to the curriculum content they seek to deliver. Accordingly, in elementary grades the teachers might focus on the intrapersonal skills and begin to emphasize the interpersonal skills of sharing and listening to the experiences and feelings of others. However, high school, undergraduate and graduate students can potentially master all of the relationship skills.

As a general approach, the authors have developed the following procedure for teaching the relationship skills:

1. State the rationale for the relationship skill.
2. Describe or define the relationship skill.
3. Model or demonstrate the relationship skill.
4. Invite learners to identify the indicators (verbal and non-verbal) of the relationship skill.
5. Invite learners in pairs to practice the relationship skill. After practicing the skill, the partners give each other constructive feedback on how the skills were implemented.
6. Invite learning pairs to reflect on their practice of the skill and discuss how the relationship skill can be applied in and outside of class.
7. Invite learners to practice the relationship skill outside of class and share their results with their peers.

Application of the Relationship Skills in Graduate Education

Over the past 30 years the first two authors have taught graduate offerings at six colleges in which the Fourth R construct was the main driving concept of the course, including "Welcome to the Fourth R," and "Human Relations in School Management." In addition, the authors have instructed courses in which the Fourth R was a major component. These graduate offerings had the following titles: "Supervision and Staff Development," "Increasing Student Responsibility and Self-Discipline in Learning Communities," and "Encouraging Skillful, Creative and Critical Thinking."

In all of these graduate courses the authors invite students to reflect upon what they have learned by using three lenses. These lenses are those of the learner, the teacher, and the staff developer. This approach encourages graduate students to imagine, internalize and understand the content from the perspective of one learning it, from the point of view of one teaching the content, and from the viewpoint of a mentor or supervisor charged with developing or growing the staff or faculty.

In repeated efforts to improve the design of the course and its associated workshops, the authors take into account quantitative ratings and qualitative feedback from participants in earlier versions, from colleagues who provide critiques and suggestions, and from observations made while monitoring groups of the participants' behavior.

To evaluate the success of the course, the authors employ all the means described above. In addition, the authors analyze participants' course projects which describe how they applied Fourth R concepts and techniques with their own students.

Summary and Conclusion

As teachers and students we are taught early and often about the importance of the 3Rs of reading, writing, and arithmetic. However, one R, the R of relating or relationships, is typically omitted. Good teaching involves the transformation of a classroom of individuals into a community of caring cooperative learners. This transformation cannot occur in isolation. It requires teachers to (a) connect with their students, and (b) empower their charges to cooperate with each other so that all can learn together. The Fourth R, the relationship skills, provides both teachers and learners with the tools to transform a group of individual learners into a caring learning community, to facilitate college and school-based change, and to mentor and supervise other professionals.

References

American Psychological Association (2015). Impact of social-emotional learning on academic achievement. *Science Daily.* American Psychological Association. Retrieved from www.sciencedaily.com/releases/2015/11/151123102813.htm

Bremer, C. D. & Smith, J. (2004). Teaching social skills. *National Center on Secondary Education and Transition, 3*(5), 1-5. Retrieved from http://www.ncset.org/publications/viewdesc.asp?id=1749

Cartledge, G. & Milburn, J. F. (1978). The case for teaching social skills in the classroom: A review. *Review of Educational Research, 1*(1), 133-156.

Lynch, S. A. & Simpson, C. G. (2010). Social skills: Laying the foundation for success. *Dimensions of Early Childhood, 38*(2), 3-12. Retrieved from http://southernearlychildhood.org/upload/pdf/Social_Skills_Laying_the_Foundation_for_Success_Sharon_A_Lynch_and_Cynthia_G_Simpson_Volume_38_Issue_2_1.pdf

Solomon, R. D. (1987). The fourth r, relating, curriculum for young adolescents. *TEAM, The Early Adolescent Magazine*, 10-14.

Solomon, R. D., Davidson, N. A. & Solomon, E. C. (1993). *The handbook for the fourth: Relationship skills, 3*. Columbia, MD: National Institute for Relationship Skills.

Solomon, R. D. (2016). The fourth r should come first. *Inservice.ASCD.org*. Retrieved from http://inservice.ascd.org/the-fourth-r-should-come-first/

Solomon, R. D. & Solomon, E. C. (1987). *The handbook for the fourth r: Relationship skills, 1*. Columbia, MD: National Institute for Relationship Training.

Solomon, R. D. & Solomon, E. C. (1987). *The handbook for the fourth r: Relationship skills, 2*. Columbia, MD: National Institute for Relationship Training.

Solomon, R. D. & Solomon, E. C. (1987). *The relationship book: The young adolescent's guide for learning the relationship skills*. Columbia, MD: National Institute for Relationship Training.

Solomon, R. D. & Solomon, E. C. (2016). What is the fourth r? *Increasing student responsibility and self-discipline within learning communities: Participant's guide* (pp. 122-159). Tucson, AZ: Fourth R Consulting.

Solomon, R. D. & Solomon, E. C. (1987). *The student's handbook for the fourth r: Relating*. Columbia, MD: National Institute for Relationship Training.

Solomon, R. D. & Davidson, N. (1990). Cooperative learning and the relationship skills: Tools for positive social development. *Cooperative Learning, 11*(2), 25-27.

Solomon, R. D. & Davidson N. (2012). What is the fourth r, the relationship skills?: *Encouraging skillful, creative and critical thinking: Participant's guide* (pp. 14-34). Tucson, AZ: Fourth R Consulting.

Solomon, R. D., Davidson, N. & Solomon, E. C. (1993). *The handbook for the Fourth r iii: Relationship activities for cooperative and collegial learning, 3*. Columbia, MD: National Institute for Relationship Training.

Solomon, R. D. & Davidson, N. (2006). Staff development in cooperative learning using cooperative structures and relationship skills. *Resources in cooperative learning* (pp. 145-147). San Juan Capistrano: Kagan Cooperative Learning.

Richard D Solomon, University of Maryland (retired)
Neil Davidson. University of Maryland, Professor Emeritus
With editing input from
Barbara J. Millis, former Director of four faculty development centers (retired).

Best Practice Teaching: What Individual and Contextual Variables Affect Who Adopts Best Practice Teaching Technology?

Imagine your primary care physician as a nice person with good bedside manner, but who is absolutely clueless and hopelessly out-of-date in regards to current evidence-based medical practice. Now imagine that you are facing a significant surgery. Would you choose your genial doctor or a more competent one to perform the surgery? In most fields, such a question is ludicrous, but in academia, we often cling to pedagogical interventions that are not supported by the research only because we have "always done it that way." Because you are reading this article, we are confident that this description does not describe you, but what factors made it more likely that you would be an adopter of such practices while others ignore them? This essay will answer two main questions: Why do some teachers implement learner-centered teaching and others do not? What individual and contextual variables affect who adopts best practice teaching?

Learner-centered teaching is an evidence-based, best practice teaching method (Richmond, et al., 2016). Many learner-centered techniques are technological in nature. Indeed, as the world becomes more technologically interdependent, the thoughtful use of technology in the classroom is critical. However, when technology is not carefully integrated into classroom, it can interfere with student learning. For example, Palak and Walls (2009) conducted a study of teachers who utilize technology in technology-rich schools. Unfortunately, the results indicated that teachers who most often utilize technology primarily employ it with the goal of easing the demands of scheduling and preparation rather than to engage students and enhance learning. Furthermore, the authors found that using technology to make a classroom more learner-centered is rare even in technology-rich schools, and is instead primarily used to enhance teacher-centered practices. For example, technology might be used to record a voice-over to a power-point presentation, which is then posted on-line for students to view, a practice with minimal research support to enhance student learning.

Palak and Walls (2009) argue that while teachers may be trained in using technology, they are rarely trained on how to integrate technology into learner-centered practices with the goal of increasing student learning. Furthermore, context matters. The few teachers who do adopt technology to promote student-centered learning typically work in schools with nearly unlimited resources and high achieving students. Thus, colleges and universities in high-density urban or isolated rural areas and who serve a wide range of student academic levels may not have the resources to use technology to support student-centered learning techniques.

In addition to contextual factors, individual professor characteristics play a role in determining the adoption of technology. Smith, Munday, and Windham (2013) examined what personality factors impact a teacher's willingness to use technology. One important characteristic is philosophical: Before any teacher can effectively implement technology, s/he must first buy-in to the overwhelming research that shows technology can improve student learning. Furthermore, "Intuitive/Thinking" types of teachers are most receptive to incorporating technology into their classrooms. These educators tend to be creative, analytical, logical, and imaginative. "Sensory/Feeling" types of educators, or those teachers who are more practical, realistic, and sociable, are least likely to be comfortable with technology.

Although research demonstrates that both individual and contextual factors can create barriers to adopting technology, these barriers are scalable and can be overcome. Ertmer, Ottenbreit-Leftwich, and York (2006) examined how some teachers were able to overcome barriers in order to implement technology to improve student learning. These researchers found that intrinsic factors such as confidence and commitment most strongly impacted successful technology use. Extrinsic factors, such as the oft-cited barriers of lack of time and resources, were less important regarding successful technology adoption.

The professor confidence required to utilize technology is, ironically, often a reflection of previous success or failure with technology. Older teachers often indicate that they struggle to utilize technology because they lack understanding and confidence to do so. To rectify this situation, teachers need opportunities to reflect on their own beliefs and practice within a supportive and collaborative environment. Peer support is often beneficial as well, as is hands-on practice. In fact, more than 75% of teachers identified workshops, seminars, or conferences as their preferred method of learning new pedagogical and technology classroom approaches (Ertmer, Ottenbreit-Leftwich, & York, 2006).

Teachers face many barriers to utilize technology in order to enhance student learning. However, the challenges we often report as most significant, including lack of time and resources, are not as critical to success as confidence and commitment. Finding institutional and personal resolve to strengthen these assets will help create classrooms that promote the learning and growth of our students. Technology is a language that is vital to communicate with the current generation of our students who are digital natives

(APA, 2011). As infants, our students swiped cell phones before they could use silverware. A primary principle of learner-centered teaching is to "meet learners where they are." As such, we need to ensure our ever-increasing fluency with technology to enhance student learning.

References

American Psychological Association. (2011). Principles for quality undergraduate education in psychology. Washington, DC. Retrieved from http://www.apa.org/education/undergrad/ principles.aspx

Ertmer, P. A., Ottenbreit-Leftwich, A., & York, C. S. (2007). Exemplary technology-using teachers: Perceptions of factors influencing success. *Journal of Computing in Teacher Education, 23*(2), 55-61.

Palak, D. & Walls, R. T. (2009). Teachers' beliefs and technology practices: A mixed-methods approach. *Journal of Research on Technology and Education, 41*(4), 417-441.

Richmond, A. S., Slattery, J. M., Mitchell, N., Morgan, R. K., & Becknell, J. (2016). Can a learner centered syllabus change students' perceptions of student-professor rapport and master teacher behaviors? *Scholarship of Teaching and Learning in Psychology, 2*(3), 159-168.

Smith, B., Munday, R., & Windham, R. (1995). Prediction of teachers' use of technology based on personality type. *Journal of Instructional Psychology, 22*(3), 281.

Anna Grace Cooper, Spalding University
Jonathan Bauman, Spalding University
DeDe Wohlfarth, Spalding University

IV. Preparing to Create SoTL: An Overview

This section features tips that focus on practical strategies for envisioning, designing, planning, and implementing SoTL projects. In other words, the authors offer perspectives on how to *do* SoTL as well as create an atmosphere conducive to such research, projects, and publications. More specifically, the authors of these tips remind us that SoTL isn't scholarly unless it's shared with the world. Before reaching that step, though, authors must plan projects effectively. As the tips in this section reveal, some SoTL projects must receive approval through your college or university's Institutional Review Board (IRB), and the process can be very specific and even time-consuming.

In addition, this section offers essays that are critical and applicable to any SoTL project, such as diversity and inclusion. The best practices for SoTL also encompass approaches for supporting faculty book groups and ways to support faculty in the SoTL process. SoTL excellence, as the tips in this section explain, takes a methodical approach and careful planning.

As you read these tips, consider ways you might apply and adapt them for use in your own SoTL projects and research. The authors here offer perspectives rooted in years of SoTL research. Learn from the experiences, observations, and approaches they share as you design a SoTL experience with your students and colleagues.

Building Institutional Support for SoTL

Institutional support is helpful, if not necessary, for publishing impactful SoTL research. If the institution places little value on SoTL research, faculty are prone to focus their research efforts elsewhere. However, even where SoTL is valued, scholars can face several challenges toward producing the types of SoTL projects that are likely to attract the interest of external funders and quality journal editorial boards. For example, any given scholar may have limited or narrow access to an adequate number and diverse array of students with whom to rigorously test a teaching approach or to investigate important learning processes. Many scholars who engage in SoTL research are educated in content knowledge of disciplines not directly related to SoTL and have limited time to master an additional domain related to education. It can also be difficult to find willing collaborators with similar interests who offer distinct sets of knowledge and experience and who have access to additional, diverse students. Investing time and energy in SoTL research can be risky when one's institution lacks the climate and resources to overcome these challenges.

Over the past two years we have been addressing such issues on an institutional level. We offer some details of our experiences to illustrate what we believe can help create a more supportive institutional environment for SoTL research. Our efforts began from the ground-up—as faculty who were interested in SoTL but who faced the types of barriers previously mentioned. We found that to have the support needed to address these barriers, we had to take action to understand and ultimately influence the university culture, catalyze existing resources, and help create new resources.

Institutional Culture

Before serious efforts were made to assess and develop resources that promote SoTL, we wanted to know the extent to which faculty and the university as an institution valued SoTL. We initially surveyed faculty about their level of interest in participating in SoTL research and in taking a leadership role in promoting and facilitating SoTL on campus. The results were very encouraging. We then identified mentions of SoTL in the university strategic plan and met with influential university administrators who confirmed that rigorous SoTL research was respected at the institutional level. We also looked for specific mentions of SoTL in the university promotion and tenure document and the university salary document, as well as parallel documents for each college and department. There appeared to be few if any official disincentives toward producing

SoTL research, though SoTL was rarely mentioned as being highly valued. We then conducted an additional survey, asking faculty about their perceptions of how well SoTL was respected at the university and in their local academic units. Though we used convenience sampling, the results were affirming.

Institutional Resources

We took some time to investigate campus resources already available that could be used to support SoTL research. Our Office of Educational Excellence was very encouraging from the beginning and has been willing to host Faculty Learning Communities that bring faculty together to learn more about SoTL and to develop SoTL projects. Our Research Design Studio, which is housed in our Teachers College and provides assistance to all faculty with research design questions, was also willing to offer their content expertise related to teaching and learning—a perfect fit for SoTL projects by faculty outside of education disciplines. University offices that provide website creation services, training and support for online teaching, and identifying and applying for grant funding were willing to support our efforts to enhance SoTL research and to accommodate a potential influx of SoTL projects. Tapping into and interconnecting existing resources is a cost-efficient way to create new avenues for obtaining university support.

Creation of New Resources

At our university faculty can form knowledge groups that focus on a common interest or project. These groups can ultimately become a center or institute after establishing a track record of productivity and value. Through the process of investigating university resources and surveying faculty, a group of faculty emerged who were willing to form a new SoTL Collaborative Initiative knowledge group. Our main objective has been to help catalyze existing resources and create new resources that help faculty form multidisciplinary, collaborative teams that produce impactful scholarship with broad application—the types of projects that tend to have appeal for funders and quality journals. We worked with university resources to have an interactive website created that above all would act as a network for interested SoTL scholars on campus to find one another. We used mass emails and attended various faculty meetings to invite faculty to create an online profile that includes searchable descriptions of their SoTL projects and interests, allowing faculty to identify and contact others with similar interests or desired expertise. The site also provides information about SoTL journals, grant opportunities, and conferences. Faculty can add to those lists of resources by submitting them through the website (managed by members of the Knowledge Group). The network is growing in membership and expanding its information and will continue to evolve.

Our efforts to address institutional support of SoTL are still in their early stages. We understand that educational institutions value scholarship more highly when it attracts external funding and publicity from high-caliber, published journal articles. Making the most of available resources and expanding the rigor and applicability of SoTL projects—through large-scale, interdisciplinary collaboration informed by a scientific knowledge base of teaching and learning—is an approach that can increase the chances of having the kind of impact that grabs the attention of the university. Such attention can lead to an increase in institutional value and resources, making the job easier for those engaging in SoTL research.

Scott S. Hall, Ball State University
David L. Largent, Ball State University
Mary Lou Vercellotti, Ball State University

Try Out Your New Pedagogy. Find Out It Works. Share It with the World. Hold on! Not So Fast...

We have likely all been there as a new instructor. We come up with a great idea for a pedagogical change, implement it, and it seems to be working. Maybe we even collect some data to see if it really does make a difference. That in and of itself is not an issue. As long as we are not doing anything unethical or illegal, full steam ahead. We are always welcome to make changes in our teaching and collect data to prove/disprove the change made a difference. Only by doing so can we be assured that it is appropriate to continue implementing our change.

So now you have found something that legitimately makes a difference. Should we keep it to ourselves so that we can be the best instructor around? Tempting as that maybe, if you are like me, you will be excited about your new-found knowledge and want to share it with others. So you mention it to some of the colleagues in your department, and they get a bit excited about it as well. You must be on to something here! You should disseminate this to a wider audience. So you start thinking about writing a manuscript, or putting together a conference presentation. You are going to let the world know about this magical pedagogical change you have discovered and become famous!

Hold on just a minute! Not so fast. Did you file a protocol with your Institutional Review Board (IRB) describing what you were going to do, who your study participants were going to be, etcetera? Did the IRB approve it? Did you get signed informed consent forms from your students (assuming that was part of the protocol)? Unless you can answer "yes" to all of those questions, you cannot ethically share your findings with anyone other than your immediate peers at your university. What you should have done—before you implemented the pedagogical change or collected data—was filed a protocol with the IRB, worked through any issues they had with it, and then followed it. Only then can you share your idea with the world and achieve fame.

The purpose of the IRB is to make sure you are not going to do anything that will injure your study participants, physically or mentally, or infringe upon their privacy. They are not there to make your life miserable, although it may seem that way at times. Rather, they are there to make sure everything is done legally and ethically. I have also found that the questions that I have to answer for my IRB protocol are the sort of things I should be considering for my study anyway. It simply makes for a better study.

Talking with others from a variety of universities, I have found that each institution's IRB behaves a bit differently, and expects slightly different things. I have the luxury of being able to work with an IRB that tends to be very helpful. If they determine what you want to do is not appropriate, they work with you to try to find an alternative that will be acceptable. I have heard of other IRBs that simply reject a protocol and leave it up to you to figure out a way to satisfy them. That can be a very frustrating guessing game!

One thing that can be particularly challenging is studying your own students. The concern is one of bias, or at least the perception of bias. If you are aware of who has agreed to participate and has not, it is possible that your actions can be biased when interacting with a given student. For example, you might give a student the benefit of the doubt when grading their paper because you know they agreed to participate. Or just the opposite, if they chose not to. I agree, few of us would actually do that—at least not intentionally—but there is the possibility that it could happen. And we don't want even the perception that it might be possible. As a result, studying one's own students presents a significant challenge.

The general wisdom is to avoid using your own students as study participants, but sometimes they are the only population that makes sense to study. For example, maybe you are the only instructor who teaches the particular class in which you want to try implementing your pedagogical change. One solution is to have a colleague conduct (parts of) the research for you. For example, your colleague can administer the informed consent forms to your students while you are out of the room and then securely hold those forms in confidence until after the semester completes and you have submitted grades for the class. In doing so, you have participants for your study, but you do not know who they are. This procedure is important so the possibility that you might treat them differently because of their participation or lack thereof is eliminated. If there are surveys (or anything else) to be administered only to the participants, your colleague again needs to do that in your absence. If the treatment is not specific to only the participants, but rather involves the entire class, then you are able to be present, and implement it yourself. Do be aware, however, that you can only include and report on data from those participants who agreed to it by signing their informed consent form.

So, dream up that new pedagogical intervention that is going to change the world of teaching. Write up your IRB protocol describing what you are going to do. Submit it to your IRB and work with them to get it approved. Implement your study. Analyze your collected data. If the data proves you were right, shout it to the world! If it did not turn out the way you thought it would, you still learned something. And it may still be worth telling the world about.

David L. Largent, Ball State University

Navigating the IRB for SoTL Research: Guidelines for the IRB Process

Should research in educational settings be held to the same standards of review as other human research? How and when is Internal Review Board (IRB) approval necessary for SoTL projects? What are the special challenges of navigating the sticky process of sharing research that was originally gathered only for classroom use? The purpose of this article is to offer a clear and ethical road map in answering these thorny questions.

What is the IRB?

The IRB seeks to ensure the rights and protection of subjects involved in research, ensure minimal risk to these individuals, and offer a neutral organization for evaluating a study's potential risks (Miser, 2005; Martin, 2014). Federal regulations dictate that all research involving human subjects must be approved by a local IRB before any data is collected (Dept. of Health and Human Services, 2009). The term "research," as used above, is often misunderstood. It is best defined as a systematic investigation designed to contribute to generalizable knowledge (Tomkowiak, 2004; Martin, 2013). Despite this clear definition, many faculty researchers are uncertain as to whether and when SoTL research requires IRB approval.

SoTL and Other Educational Research

Faculty are embracing new roles as both educators and investigators, as the development of innovative and effective new curricula requires extensive experimentation. This situation often results in continuous data collection by faculty members in their own classrooms. Once the evidence supports these innovations, then the results should be shared with other institutions (Tomkowiak, 2004). Educational researchers ascribe to the notion of "academic freedom" in classrooms, and do not consider within-classroom research to require ethical review (Martin, 2014). However, while student data collection is common for internal curriculum improvement, once researchers make a decision to share their findings through either publication or presentation (making it generalizable knowledge), their study requires IRB approval (Tomkowiak, 2004; Miser, 2005). For example, an eager professor enacts a new curriculum in his class. He assesses its effectiveness through student surveys and finds it to be wildly successful. So, he decides to share his findings at a local conference. Without intending to do so, he would have conducted research with human subjects without the necessary IRB approval.

Even without the intent to publish, many educationally based research projects still face ethical issues, as the methodology required to investigate student performance often involves human participation, observation, and evaluation. Each of these data-collection methods poses risks to students (Tomkowiak, 2004). In fact, students are often considered a "vulnerable population" because their class grade and future recommendation letters could be influenced by their willingness to participate in a faculty member's research study. The power differential between professors and students may inhibit some learners' ability to decline participation. Furthermore, SoTL research often relies on sensitive student data, such as student journals or personal conversations. All of these factors mean that student subjects are at risk when participating in educational research, perhaps even beyond the designation of "minimal risk." For this reason, academic studies using student participants must adhere to many of the same ethical standards as medical research (Miser, 2005).

Navigating the IRB

Although IRB guidelines vary by institution, they share three common characteristics. All IRBs require some form of ethics training and certificate documentation, approval of a study from a local review board, and annual follow up reviews with addendums (Martin, 2013). Studies may be approved on three separate levels of IRB review: full board, expedited, or exempt. Researchers must determine what level of review their project will require prior to submitting documentation. Most SoTL research will meet the necessary qualifications for expedited or exempt review, meaning the approval process may be shorter. In order for research to be exempt, it must pose minimal risk to human subjects and guarantee the confidential protection of private information (Miser, 2005). The accompanying chart is helpful in determining what level of review is indicated for a professor's SoTL research (Types of IRB Review, n.d.).

In order to meet the criteria of "educational research" under the "Exempt" category, a study must be conducted in an educational setting and follow normal educational practices, such as effectiveness/comparison studies of curricula. Surveys, interviews,

Levels of IRB Review

Full Board	Expedited	Exempt
More than "minimal risk" to subjects Not covered under other review categories	Not greater than minimal risk Fits one of the Expedited Review Categories	Less than "minimal risk" Fits one of the Exempt Categories

Exempt Categories:
1. Education research
2. Surveys, interviews, educational tests, public observations (that do not involve children)
3. Studies of public officials
4. Analysis of previously-collected, anonymous data
5. Public benefit or service program
6. Consumer acceptance, taste, and food quality studies

Expedited Categories:
1. Clinical studies of drugs and medical devices only when certain conditions are met
2. Collection of blood samples in certain populations and within certain amounts
3. Prospective collection of biological specimens for research purposes by noninvasive means
4. Collection of data through noninvasive procedures routinely employed in medical clinical practice
5. Research involving materials (data, documents, records, or specimens) that have been collected, or will be collected solely for non-research purposes
6. Collection of data from voice, video, digital, or image recordings made for research purposes
7. Research on individual or group characteristics or behavior or research employing survey, interview, oral history, focus group, program evaluation, human factors evaluation, or quality assurance methodologies

and public observations are also exempt from a full IRB review. Studies that involve analyzing previously collected, anonymous data, such as exam grades and essays, are also generally exempt from a full board review.

Although most SoTL research will be deemed exempt, faculty researchers must still go through the IRB process. Faculty members cannot decide on their own whether their research will be deemed exempt (Tomkowiak, 2004; Miser, 2005). Studies that will certainly trigger a full board review include those that involve research where participants are identifiably recorded, are asked embarrassing or compromising questions, or receive a benefit, such as class credit, for participating (Tomkowiak, 2004; Miser, 2005). Suggestions to minimize risk include offering equivalent alternatives to participation, and actively working to minimize the inherent power differential between students and professors in SoTL research. Researching educators must ensure their data will be collected in a way that protects their students' confidentiality and obtains their informed consent. If these guidelines are followed, exciting and innovative new practices can be freely shared.

References

Martin, R. C. (2013). Navigating the IRB: The ethics of SoTL. *New Directions for Teaching and Learning, 2013*(136), 59-71.

Martin, R. C., Gurung, R., & Wilson, J. (2014). *IRBs and research on teaching and learning.* Office of Teaching Resources in Psychology. Retrieved from http://teachpsych.org/Resources/Documents/otrp/resources/martin14.pdf

Miser, W. F. (2005). Educational research—to IRB, or not to IRB. *Fam Med, 37*(3), 168-173.

National Commission for the Protection of Human Subjects of Biomedical and Behavioral Research (1979). *The Belmont Report: Ethical principles and guidelines for the protection of human subjects of research.* Washington, DC: U.S. Government Printing Office.

Tomkowiak, J. M., & Gunderson, A. J. (2004). To IRB or not to IRB? *Academic Medicine, 79*(7), 628-632.

Types of IRB Review. (n.d.). OPRS Office for the Protection of Research Subjects. *University of Southern California.* Retrieved from http://oprs.usc.edu/review/typesofirb/

US Department of Health and Human Services. (2009). *Code of federal regulations.* Title 45 Public Welfare. Department of Health and Human Services. Part 46: Protection of human subjects. Retrieved from https://www.hhs.gov/ohrp/sites/default/files/ohrp/policy/ohrpregulations.pdf

Catherine Thompson, Spalding University
Lauren Holder, Spalding University
DeDe Wohlfarth, Spalding University

How SoTL Can Work for You

New faculty at colleges and universities settle into a number of roles and responsibilities and can find the many obligations they face render the total completion of their research and scholarship agendas quite difficult. This situation can be particularly true at institutions that are teaching centered with heavy teaching loads and service components. For this reason, it makes perfect sense to consider scholarship on teaching and learning to achieve professional development, better teaching, and scholarly publications. Not only can investigation into teaching and student learning make for publishable research, it also enhances our classroom strategies and can increase student learning. In that way, one might choose to elaborate on a professional development activity or an innovative approach to teaching their discipline in a scholarly publication thereby achieving multiple levels of contributions to the profession. In what follows, I will discuss how publications related to classroom innovation and pedagogical methods aided me to strengthen my application for tenure and promotion and make a case for anyone to consider SoTL.

First off, for those unfamiliar with the topic, SoTL involves a close look at teaching strategies and their impact on student learning and can easily lead to awareness of self, of students, and provide input from other colleagues and scholars. According to Hutchings, Huber, and Ciccone (2011, p. xix), "the scholarship of teaching and learning encompasses a broad set of practices that engage teachers in looking closely and critically at student learning in order to improve their own courses and programs, and to share insights with other educators who can evaluate and build on their efforts." I teach all levels of French language and culture, which is a discipline that easily lends itself to SoTL with the inherent focus on pedagogy for facilitating language learning, but the openness of the topic makes it easy to apply knowledge of and practice in any discipline. I regularly attend conferences focused on teaching such as the Kentucky World Language Association (KWLA), American Council on Teaching Foreign Languages (ACTFL), Central States (CSCTFL), which allows me to hear about new trends in pedagogy and also reflect on how I can implement lessons learned in my own teaching. I have been able to meet and interact with colleagues to discuss best practices that provide insights and invigoration for teachers. Through these meetings, one can identify individuals with similar interests and with whom projects and studies can be conducted.

SoTL can also be extremely practical for building a list of scholarly work. At my university, we teach four classes per semester, so teaching is regarded as the most important factor in earning tenure and promotion. In my application for tenure, I had one peer reviewed article published related to my area of doctoral training. However, the rest of my scholarly work came in large part from book reviews on pedagogical methods and materials and articles on classroom teaching. Of those articles, two of them came directly from practice. One related to online learning and was a summary of lessons learned in an eight week course on online teaching in which I participated through our instructional design unit. This article was the perfect marriage of teaching, professional development, and scholarship. In that way, I was able to include three of the four areas of evaluation. The second work came from a lesson that I had created and used in my class. Basically, I crafted an article that explained my approach to teaching students to read authentic materials in French. The details of the lesson provided pre-reading, reading, and post-reading tasks as well as ideas for expanding on the lesson for cultural content and context. These are simple ways to turn our professional development and teaching activities into publishable research.

If you are not familiar with SoTL or have not considered such research as a way to improve teaching all the while engaging in scholarly work, it is a great way to accomplish several goals with one project. If you are interested in learning more, some suggestions would be as follows.

- Explore the resources on your campus. Does your school have a center for teaching and learning? Are there colleagues on your campus who engage in SoTL?
- Explore the literature.
- Find out if there is a SoTL outlet for your discipline (peer-reviewed journal, collection of teaching tips, etc.).
- Approach professional development as a way to accomplish multiple endeavors.
- Participate in Institutional Review Board (IRB) training. This element is important if analyses of human subjects are presented in your scholarship. Their website is a good starting point: https://www.hhs.gov/ohrp/register-irbs-and-obtain-fwas/irb-registration/index.html

In sum, SoTL can be a fun, fulfilling, and dynamic way to become a better teacher and make progress toward tenure and promotion. Give it a try!

Reference

Hutchings, P., Huber, M., & Ciccone, A. (2011). *The scholarship of teaching and learning reconsidered.* San Francisco, CA: Jossey-Bass.

Randi Polk, Eastern Kentucky University

Why Not Study Syllabi? Conduct High Quality Research on What You Already Know and Do

I (Nate Mitchell) regularly supervise doctoral students on their dissertations. Students often ask, "What should I research?" My most frequent answer is, "Study your passion and/or study what you know." If you are interested in the SoTL field, I assume one of your passions is postsecondary high quality teaching. The next step is identifying something to research that you might already be doing which impacts learning outcomes. To that end, we suggest studying syllabi.

Why syllabi? You may not have thought of syllabi as important, research-worthy, sources of study, but consider the following. First, many of you are likely required to develop your own syllabus, so you are already fairly familiar with syllabi and have easy access to syllabi that could be researched. Second, as a result of participant feedback from syllabus presentations, it's clear that many faculty are surprised syllabus development has empirical support and that many classroom problems can be reduced or even eliminated through a carefully written syllabus. This situation suggests that readers might be interested in this topic and that this would be a productive area of research.

Intrigued by the notion of studying syllabi? A good place to start is by looking at current research on syllabi. As reported by Slattery and Carlson (2005), the syllabus serves multiple purposes: sets the tone for your entire semester, motivates students to set ambitious but reasonable goals, allows faculty to plan their semester, allows students to structure their work across the semester, and provides a 'contract' between faculty and students. Starting with this foundation leads to multiple questions that can be asked about syllabi. For example,

- What are your students' perceptions of your syllabus? What did they find helpful? What did they find unclear? Do outcomes and perceptions change when you make changes to your syllabus?
- Does your syllabus set the tone you intend? Why not study the perceived tone?
- Are your students reading the syllabus? Are there differences in course outcomes between those who read it and those who don't?
- Do you teach more than one section of an identical course? Consider changing

an aspect of the syllabus in just one section and measure some interesting outcome between courses.

Of course, as you develop your syllabus questions, review the literature to ensure that you're familiar with other research on the same topic. Even if someone has addressed the same question, minor modifications can lead you to a productive study. Further, as you engage in the process of mining the literature for research ideas for your own study, you may find ideas for improving your current teaching. A win-win situation for you and your students.

Reference

Slattery, J. M., & Carlson, J. F. (2005). Preparing an effective syllabus: Current best practices. *College Teaching, 53*(4), 159-164.

Nate Mitchell, Spalding University
Robin K. Morgan, Indiana University Southeast

Taking Steps to Control Variables in a Quantitative Quasi-Experiment

When I was inspired to do SoTL research, I was scheduled to teach two sections of a course—a great SoTL research opportunity. I tend to do quantitative research in my field, and I wanted to apply that experience to investigate learning gain differences between sections. There are some challenges to conducting quantitative, hypothesis-testing SoTL research because classroom research is messy. I took a number of steps to strengthen my research design in order to control as many variables as possible, save for the independent variable. The semester before the research, I piloted the methods, materials, and measures. During the data collection, I matched the student experience in the two sections as much as possible. Both sections of the course were taught by the same instructor, with the same textbook, using the same pedagogy, activities, assessments, following the same schedule.

We cannot, however, control who enrolls into our course or into the sections of our course. Since we generally cannot assign students to a particular section or group, we have to think creatively to enact some experimental control. How can we "randomize" groups when students self-enroll? There are a few steps we can take with the course schedule, meeting times, and location.

The course schedule and the class meeting times might trigger differences in the student population in the two sections. For instance, students who enroll first (based on number of credits or intrinsic motivation) might fill the section at a more desirable time. In my case, one section was scheduled for 75-minute class meetings twice a week (Tuesdays and Thursdays) in the early afternoon. I requested that the other section also be scheduled as 75-minute class meetings twice a week (Mondays and Wednesdays) in the early afternoon. This schedule change required special permission because of the university's preference to fill classroom space most efficiently, but the request was approved because the reason for the request (SoTL research) was valid. Additionally, making the course schedule parallel seemed to have helped to equalize the enrollment number in each section, avoiding a full section at a preferred day and time and an under-enrolled sections at a less preferred class meeting schedule. Additionally, having the physical room equally as "full" makes the learning environments more similar. Having even section enrollment strengthens the conclusions that can be drawn from comparisons between sections.

Also, while students were enrolling, the course section information did not list the location of the class meeting. This small adjustment increases the chances that each section will draw equally from the general student population. For instance, one building location might appeal to specific majors for the classroom's proximity to the department "home." In my research, I wanted to investigate if the classroom context impacted learning outcomes, comparing active learning pedagogy in a traditional classroom versus in a newly-designed interactive learning space classroom. If the students could see the section's classroom, it is possible that interested, highly motivated students might have disproportionally enrolled in the innovative classroom context.

Another important aspect of instructor-as-researcher SoTL is how to measure student outcomes. Instructor-as-researchers have to address the potential for bias when using course grades. Instructor grades may be biased because course grades are not blind to the experimental context, and the instructors' own feelings about the context could subconsciously influence course grades. One option is to assess student performance blindly (e.g., Day & Foley, 2006). For this research, I chose to use an external measure of course knowledge as a pre- and post-test. After finding a free, external measure of the skills aligned with the course objectives, I arranged for the students to take the test as a pretest during the first week of the course and a post-test at the end of the course. The external test was set up as a random pool of questions, meaning that students do not get the same questions. This feature also insures that the instructor-as-researcher cannot "teach to the test." The external measure also showed how the skills learned in the course had merit in the "real" world simply because it was created and used by the public. In my opinion, the use of a pretest had a pedagogical value as formative assessment. And, of course, the results served as an opportunity for the students to realize the change in their content knowledge. Measuring learning gains (change in score) rather than using the post-test score also controls for differences in initial content knowledge.

In this research study, I also asked the students about their perceptions of the course with Likert scale questions. For instance, I asked to what extent active learning pedagogy was enacted in each section of the course. The students also had the opportunity to respond to open-ended questions. For instance, the students explained what course design features were most useful for their own learning. These data supported the quantitative findings and led to a published research article (Vercellotti, forthcoming). By taking steps to minimize variables, which are numerous in classroom research, we can complete robust quantitative hypothesis-testing SoTL research.

References

Day, J. A. & Foley, J. D. (2006). Evaluating a web lecture intervention in a human-computer interaction course. *IEEE Transactions on Education, 49*(4), 420-431.

Vercellotti, M. L. (*forthcoming*). Do interactive learning spaces increase student achievement? A comparison of classroom context. *Active Learning in Higher Education*.

Mary Lou Vercellotti, Ball State University

Research Support Faculty Fellow

At our university, SoTL has been encouraged with faculty development initiatives, including faculty-to-faculty support. Research Support Faculty Fellows are faculty members who provide additional assistance, such as leading seminars or workshops as well as providing individual support for SoTL. The fellowship has included a reduced teaching load. As the first Research Support Faculty Fellow at my university, I have discovered that I have three main roles: SoTL researcher example, SoTL resource, and SoTL intermediary.

SoTL Researcher Example

As a faculty member who has added SoTL research to my research agenda, I show that it is possible. Simply sharing my SoTL experience, especially with incoming faculty, also demystifies the process. SoTL is not just done by "SoTL" faculty or faculty in certain disciplines. I promote attendance (and presenting at) SoTL conferences, through my own attendance and sharing innovative ideas when I return. Seeing the wide variety of SoTL possibilities can transform a faculty member's understanding of SoTL from a nebulous concept to a tangible professional goal. Further, as an example of a SoTL researcher, I dispel the notion that we do not have time for SoTL. At our university, SoTL publications "count" as part of scholarship requirements during our annual review. Really, SoTL allows us to double-count our efforts because our undertaking of reviewing teaching effectiveness improves our teaching and increases our scholarship output. I also think that when we are intentional about our goals, our participation in SoTL research is a valuable metacognitive exercise which improves our teaching and scholarship more generally.

SoTL Resource

I have created a space for faculty to discuss SoTL, particularly research design. One forum was a research workshop series, which was held over five weeks during the summer. The workshop sessions were (mostly) self-contained so that attendance in the previous sessions was not required. The purpose of the three-part workshop was to break down the steps of designing a research study into doable actions.

The goal of the first session was simply to get the research ball rolling by setting a research goal, including a timeline. Using a worksheet, we started with when the data would be collected and worked backwards. Data collection often has timing constraints while the start of a research project is vague and, therefore, not urgent on our "to-do" list. For instance, we might have a plan to collect data during a particular semester while we are teaching a particular course or introducing a teaching innovation. Working backward from the data collection time frame, we added the necessary steps (e.g., finalization of instruments and plan, review of the literature) to arrive at a practical start date. Workshop participants then formulated a draft research question. I gave some examples of SoTL research being done on campus to begin the discussion, and everyone shared research ideas. Then the participants considered an appropriate forum for their SoTL, perhaps a field-specific journal or a cross-disciplinary SoTL journal. I shared a compiled list of general SoTL journals and posted to our university's SoTL Collaboration Initiative knowledge group website. Through the process, we realized that with the many and varied demands on our time, we have to intentionally plan SoTL.

During the second session, participants delved deeper into research design using active, collaborative discussion. Participants wrote their potential research question on one side of hand-held whiteboards. On the other side of the whiteboard, participants wrote what evidence would be needed to answer that question. Potential data sources included: descriptions (e.g., observations, reflections), opinions (e.g., surveys, interviews), learning outcomes (e.g., pretest/posttest results, external evaluations). After an open discussion of each question, I probed further by asking what a skeptical reader might what to know. For instance, can the findings be explained by another variable? The process may also help to refine the research question(s). The group setting offered the added value of brainstorming and peer-feedback on each research design.

With a plan for the research, the focus of the third workshop turned to determining whether the research required oversight from the Institutional Review Board (IRB). This step can often seem onerous. To elucidate the process, we reviewed examples of successful human subject research applications and consent forms.

I have offered faculty the opportunity for individual meetings throughout the year, as scheduled appointment and also during walk-in hours. As a SoTL resource, I try to ask questions that allow the faculty member to evaluate their research design. I might ask questions about which demographic information might be important to gather. A common suggestion has been to incorporate a "test" or survey to serve as a baseline to measure change over time, for instance, of how student attitudes might change during/after the course.

SoTL Intermediary

The need for an intermediary may arise with the IRB, especially with instructor-as-researcher SoTL. At our university, our role as instructor must remain separate from our role as researcher. We must make a valid argument to the IRB of why we want to conduct research in our own courses. (One reason is that we are in a unique position to understand the dynamics of our course.) Our students should never feel coerced into participating in an instructor's research project. Another issue is that the integrity of our grades can be questioned if we mix our roles. Therefore, an intermediary can facilitate the research consent procedure required by the IRB so that the course instructor does not know which students consented to participate and which have not, avoiding even the appearance of coercion or bias.

A research support faculty fellow can successfully support SoTL as faculty example, as a resource, and as an intermediary. As with our teaching, being intentional with our SoTL often leads to greater success.

Mary Lou Vercellotti, Ball State University

Read and Replicate: Two Necessary Activities for Teaching and SoTL Excellence

Step 1: READ

So you want to stay sharp as an instructor in higher education. If so, you need to schedule time to read the current literature. If you are reading this teaching tip, you are taking the first step! There is never enough time in higher education to do everything you want or is expected of you. However, if you are reading this text, you probably care deeply about high quality teaching. Taking time to read current SoTL literature is a must. Just as you would hope your physician is up to date with the current empirically supported techniques, your students have a right to expect you to be up to date with the current, empirically supported techniques in higher education instruction.

You might think you are doing what you are supposed to in the classroom, but are you sure?

- Advances in both the broad and discipline-specific SoTL fields happen frequently. Further, as technology continues to advance at exponential rates, what you learned five years ago may no longer be relevant.

Finding current SoTL literature may be easier than you think. Since you are probably used to reading discipline-based journals, you may be comforted to hear that almost every discipline now has a teaching related journal. For example, psychology has long benefited from the journal, the *Teaching of Psychology*. However, you will miss much of the SoTL literature if you do not look outside your discipline. Here are some examples of journals and resources which have been helpful to us over the years.

- *Journal of the Scholarship of Teaching and Learning*
- *Journal on Excellence in College Teaching*
- *College Teaching*
- *Chronicle of Higher Education*

We recommend that you schedule a meeting with yourself to read the literature. If you are like us, if it is not a meeting on the calendar, it is not likely to happen. Therefore, we suggest that you put a weekly SoTL Meeting on your calendar. Further, you can tell colleagues and students, "I'm sorry, I have a meeting to attend." They don't need to know that it is a meeting with your favorite journal or favorite edition of the *It Works for Me* series!

Step 2: REPLICATE

If you have been reading the current literature, then you are likely applying ideas in the classroom from articles or books. If you are trying the techniques presented in the research articles in your own classroom, why not replicate the study? Chances are you are teaching a different course or a different student population, or a different format (F2F, hybrid, etc.). There is no reason to stall a SoTL research project because you don't know how to proceed or what to study. Start immediately with replication! Use similar methodology to the research articles from which you "stole" your latest teaching technique. Chances are the authors of the original article are willing to share ideas/lessons learned, survey instruments, etc. and support your endeavors. The data you collect will likely be welcome for presentation at SoTL conferences and worthy of publication. You may not "change the SoTL world" with your replication study. However, you will gain invaluable experience in developing SoTL methodology and might just end up with SoTL presentations and a SoTL publication or two. Of course, if you decide to collect data, check with your institution's policies about IRB approval.

Nate Mitchell, Spalding University
Robin K. Morgan, Indiana University Southeast

Faculty Book Group on the Scholarship of Teaching and Learning

Faculty book groups exist in various forms. Whereas some groups are self-organizing, others are formally supported by the administration (e.g., Scourfield & Taylor, 2014). Groups may choose to read fiction (e.g., Alsop, 2015; Beach & Yussen, 2011) or only scholarly research. Book discussions are led in various ways, ranging from designated facilitators to equal discussion roles across all members. Potential benefits to book group participation include increased intentional reflection on current teaching practices (e.g., White, 2016), instrumental formal and informal networking opportunities (e.g.,

Alsop, 2015), professional self-discovery (e.g., Long, 2003), and personal validation and support (e.g., Macoun & Miller, 2014).

Five years ago, my colleagues and I formed a book group focused on the scholarship of teaching and learning (SoTL). Our group is comprised of five faculty members representing four disciplines: education, English, history, and psychology. When we initially formed our group, our loosely stated goals included collaborative learning about teaching and providing support for one another. We wanted to learn new teaching strategies from both published research and each other. We also wanted to help one another through teaching struggles and celebrate each other's classroom successes.

Before the beginning of each semester, members distribute general descriptions of SoTL books we think would meet our goals. We avoid books with content that significantly overlaps that of books we have already read. After voting by email on which book we most want to read, we divide that book into four or five parts. Approximately every month we meet over lunch to discuss the assigned chapters and share how they relate to experiences with our students. This design allows us to benefit from discussing the SoTL research as well as to the ways it directly applies to our specific campus and student population. For example, reading *Teaching What You Don't Know* by Therese Huston (2012) provided those of us who teach a required freshmen interdisciplinary course with beneficial strategies and insights when teaching material outside our specific discipline. Our discussion format is conversational and spontaneous; we do not assign facilitator or leader roles.

Our group has discussed a variety of books about teaching and learning. These books have focused on student learning (Ambrose, Bridges, DiPietro, & Lovett, 2010), critical thinking (Brookfield, 2012), student engagement (Barkley, 2009), intentional teaching (Berg & Seeber, 2016), and best practices for teaching and scholarship (Bain, 2011; Chambliss & Takacs, 2014). One semester we strayed from our SoTL focus by reading *Give and Take* by Adam Grant (2014). Through this book, we discussed the importance of looking outside ourselves and focusing on what we can do to support others, ranging from sharing our resources and ideas with others, as well as serving as mentors.

Our initial goals for the book club are continually being met, and the benefits we have received have exceeded our initial expectations. Having a book group focused on the scholarship of teaching and learning has helped provide us with ideas and support needed to become more effective professors. Based on our book group experience, I encourage other instructors to form SoTL book clubs and reap the benefits that we have.

References

Alsop, R. (2015). A novel alternative. Book groups, women, and workplace networking. *Women's Studies International Forum, 52*, 30-38.

Ambrose, S. A., Bridges, M. W., DiPietro, M., & Lovett, M. C. (2010). *How learning works: Seven research-based principles for smart teaching.* San Francisco, CA: John Wiley & Sons.

Bain, K. (2011). *What the best college teachers do.* Cambridge, MA: Harvard University Press.

Barkley, E. F. (2009*). Student engagement techniques: A handbook for college faculty.* San Francisco, CA: John Wiley & Sons.

Beach, R., & Yussen, S. (2011). Practices of productive adult book clubs. *Journal of Adolescent and Adult Literacy, 55*(2), 121-131.

Berg, M., & Seeber, B. K. (2016). *The slow professor: Challenging the culture of speed in the academy.* Canada: University of Toronto Press.

Brookfield, S. D. (2012). *Teaching for critical thinking: Tools and techniques to help students question their assumptions.* San Francisco, CA: John Wiley & Sons.

Chambliss, D. F., & Takacs, C. G. (2014). *How college works.* Cambridge, MA: Harvard University Press.

Grant, A. M. (2014). *Give and take: A revolutionary approach to success.* New York, NY: Penguin Books.

Huston, T. (2012). *Teaching what you don't know.* Cambridge, MA: Harvard University Press.

Long, E. (2003). *Book clubs: Women and the uses of reading in everyday life.* Chicago, IL: The University of Chicago Press.

Macoun, A., & Miller, D. (2014). Surviving (thriving) in academic: Feminist support networks and women ECRs. *Journal of Gender Studies, 23*(3), 287-301.

Scourfield, J., & Taylor, A. (2014). Using a book group to facilitate student learning about social work. *Social Work Education, 33*(4), 533-538.

White, K. M. (2016). Professional development that promotes powerful interactions: Using teacher book clubs to reflect on quality in teacher-child relationships. *Dimensions of Early Childhood, 44*(3), 28-34.

Karyn S. McKenzie, Georgetown College

Reflection as Transition Between Sequential Courses: The Focused Autobiographical Sketch

This tip is meant to demonstrate how SoTL research can lead to faculty collaboration within an academic program. Design of SoTL research intended for implementation in one course can have outcomes that impact learning in a subsequent course. A key may be communication with the faculty colleague teaching the next course in the academic program about both the research and teaching strategies applied as part of it. This communication can not only provide support for the research, it may develop a bridge to link content of two courses together, scaffolding content within a program. The example provided describes a series of sequential reflection prompts for a required field experience component in one course that is revisited in the next course in the program.

Field experience in any discipline provides students opportunity to know their chosen field at a deeper level. Students observe and interact within a professional setting, connected to course objectives. The research question that guided this study was: *How can instructors coach students to reflect deeper, beyond recall of an experience?* The qualitative study includes analysis of data collected through student reflection journals and presentations, surveys, and other evaluative tools. Contextual factors such as integration, collaboration, and partnerships can provide reciprocity for external stakeholders hosting university students.

Through a series of ten reflection journal prompts, students were asked to observe and write about their weekly experiences in the field. The prompts began fairly general and became more specific. The journal was collected multiple times throughout the semester. Phrases were highlighted and questions posed within the text for students to respond to, in an attempt to deepen reflective writing. Students were expected to address the questions and resubmit their revisions. John Dewey's four criteria for reflection (Rodgers, 2002) were introduced to students. To communicate differentiation of depth of reflective writing to students, we presented Lee's (2005) levels of recall, rationalization, and reflectivity (R1, R2 and R3). This strategy could be used in any course with a field experience component.

My colleague and I were in the midst of redesigning curriculum for our program during the initial data collection phase of this SoTL research. We sought ways to connect course content, and extend and expand on student experiences from previous courses, deepening potential for learning. At the end of this course, students used their journal reflections as the basis for their final presentation. The final journal prompt was the focused autobiographical sketch, which was assigned after completion of field experience.

The focused autobiographical sketch is a classroom assessment technique (CAT) intended as a formative assessment to be implemented in the beginning of a course. In this instance, as the final reflection in a junior-level course, it was then used in part as the entry point for the next course in the sequence of the major. The prompt was:

> In 15-20 minutes, write in your reflection journal about the impact of your field experience this semester. How has this experience affected you? What have you learned about yourself and about the field? What have you learned about [course content / course goals] from your experience at [experiential learning site]? What will you take away from the experience?

According to Angelo and Cross (1993), the focused autobiographical sketch is a technique for assessing students' awareness of attitudes and values. It is considered a medium difficulty level assessment due to the time it takes to evaluate and instructor effort to determine how to best incorporate students' experiences into course content, creating more student-centered instruction. These factors change the course each time it is taught, tailoring to the needs and experiences of the particular students.

The focused autobiographical sketch aided students in developing their final presentation for the course, which became a tool to link two sequential classes together. It provided a natural and seamless flow between courses. As faculty, we became more aware and interested in each other's course content and objectives. There are many benefits of communicating with colleagues about SoTL research. In this case, I recognized benefits relative to consistency in teaching students to document and reflect on their experiences in the field as well as reflecting together as colleagues on our own teaching practice.

My colleague and I are intentional about how we teach students to document and reflect on their experiences in the field. While implementing my SoTL research, I became more motivated to discuss with my colleague strategies of teaching students to document and reflect on their field experiences. We acknowledged ways to scaffold expectations of student reflections in different courses. Strands of professional development are woven into the courses as students are taught how to document and reflect on their own journey towards professionalism. It is hoped that as students increase skill level in reflective writing, they will become more effective practitioners in their field.

If it is a priority to teach reflective practice within a program (and embark in SoTL research about it), it is advantageous to reflect together as colleagues on the process. Directing attention to both how we teach reflective practice to our students as well as how we engage in our own reflective practice might strengthen how personal and professional identities develop, both in our students and in ourselves.

It may be possible to increase faculty morale and job satisfaction when faculty can come to a shared vision relative to a classroom assessment technique that traverse courses. When faculty colleagues more fully understand one another's courses, the consistency of messaging when representing the program—within the department and across the university—may be strengthened.

References

Angelo, T. A., & Cross, K. P. (1993). *Classroom assessment techniques: A handbook for college teachers* (2nd ed.). San Francisco, CA: Jossey-Bass.

Lee, H. (2005). Understanding and assessing preservice teachers' reflective thinking. *Teaching and Teacher Education, 21,* 699-715.

Rodgers, C. (2002). Defining reflection: Another look at John Dewey and reflective thinking. *Teachers College Record, 104*(4), 842-866.

Stephanie Danker, Miami University (Oxford, OH)

A Blueprint to Encourage Student Writing

This essay will share practical advice on how to teach students to write better, whether in the context of helping with Scholarship of Teaching and Learning research or for class assignments. First, however, I would like to share a story. Over the last two years, I (Wohlfarth) have watched as my talented sister and her hard-working husband build a beautiful home from scratch. She is an architect by trade; he is a master carpenter/electrician. They chose a beautiful 5-acre wooded plot overlooking a river to build their craftsman style house. Week by week, I watched as a house emerged from a grassy clearing beside the steep hill of a densely wooded forest. They bought a bulldozer, moved rocks the size of Volkswagens, and the grassy clearing became an excavated cave. They laid the foundation, moved heavy beams in place, and eventually, the wooden frame of the dwelling-to-be was silhouetted against the sky like a child's simple first line drawing of a house. They framed the house for months, with each week bringing a new surprise: trusses for the roof, exterior walls, holes for future windows. Eventually, the walled-in house allowed them to work in the dry interior of what would become their home.

I am not as talented as my sister and brother-in-law, but I read *This Old House* magazine, watch HGTV's Chip and Jo, and am handy with a planer, miter saw, and drill. Imagine, if you will, how it might have played out if I, little pink toolbox in hand, volunteered to add window trim when the house had no windows or walls. Imagine if I had cut the boards, mitered the edges, and used my super-addictive nail gun to attach my newly created trim to a non-existent wall.

My sister and brother-in-law are patient people, but such "help" would have been unnecessary, disruptive, and impeded progress.

Extend this analogy to teaching students how to write. When we provide ill-timed, detail-oriented feedback on student papers, we replicate the window trim mistake. I have often made this mistake. I am the academic queen of carrying my little pink tool box into dangerous hard-hat-only construction areas—papers that needed massive work to be structurally sound. In other words, I have repeatedly given students line-by-line feedback despite knowing their papers were disasters. My misguided efforts revealed my faulty underlying paradigm.

Like many of you, I understand that writing is an active learning strategy that greatly aids student learning, regardless of course discipline or content (Bean, 2011). Research supports that both low-stakes and high-stakes writing assignments help students learn. So I assigned fun, short, informal low-stakes assignments and big, fat, juicy high-stakes papers. Yet when I read student papers, I bemoaned their quality. I was frustrated by blatant grammar violations, numerous misspellings, haphazard organization, and indiscernible thesis statements. I wondered how some students ever passed high school freshman English. After all, I reasoned, if students cannot write a sentence, then they cannot write a paragraph, and in turn cannot write a paper.

Actually, the opposite is true. If students cannot write a paper, then they cannot write a paragraph, then they cannot write a sentence. In other words, if a paper has no thesis, then it cannot be organized. If it is not organized, then its individual sentences will be nonsensical. So, my detailed, extensive, line-by-line feedback, delineating their numerous grammar mistakes, detracted from the more important global feedback that needed to hear: they had no organizing blueprint.

No wonder it seemed as though students hadn't read my feedback on the first draft as they turned in their second drafts. No wonder they continued to make the same mistakes. Suddenly, I understood why I had a stack of vintage term papers in my office that students had never bothered to pick up. My feedback was not helpful—they were not learning from it. In fact, my comments were disruptive, unnecessary, and impeded progress and, contributing to the problem that I was trying to solve.

My stack of unreturned term papers is no longer growing because I follow this useful advice, culled from listening to wiser colleagues and reading books like Bean's *Engaging Ideas*:

1. When beginning to grade a student paper, quickly glance at the whole paper before you carefully read it from top to bottom. Can you identify a clear thesis? If not, don't read the entire paper line-by-line. Instead, provide 2-3 sentences of overall feedback about the paper's structural problem. Rubrics can help organize your feedback as well.
2. Fight the urge to identify sentence-level errors when grading and instead focus on the "big picture." Tailor your feedback to match the overall "stage" of the students' writing. Detail-oriented, line-by-line feedback can be helpful, but only if the paper is already in excellent shape. Remember, window trim only matters when the foundation has already been built.
3. Encourage rewriting. Even the best authors do not write spotless prose on their first efforts. If we want quality writing from students, we have to avoid the frantic 24-hour-dash-to-deadline, when students sit down at their computers, or perhaps their cell phones, and write a paper due tomorrow from scratch. Multiple deadlines to encourage rewriting sounds like more work grading papers, but this is not necessarily true if we grade strategically.
4. Students need feedback not just from professors, but from classmates and peer mentors at your university writing center. Scaffold assignments to ensure that students are rewarded for seeking such feedback.
5. Consider alternative methods of providing feedback, such as voice recording your feedback into your cell phone and emailing it to students, which can be more efficient than writing or typing.
6. Adopt the philosophy that teaching writing is not just the responsibility of our colleagues in the English department, but our shared academic responsibility. Like the house analogy, let's work together to create something beautiful. Just leave your pink toolbox at home until the walls are built.

Reference

Bean, J. C. (2011). *Engaging ideas: The professor's guide to integrating writing, critical thinking, and active learning in the classroom* (2nd ed.). San Francisco, CA: Jossey Bass.

DeDe Wohlfarth, Spalding University
Lauren Holder, Spalding University
Catherine Thompson, Spalding University
Paul Morgan, Spalding University

Teaching Tips as a Means of SoTL Scholarship: Yes, Write Some Tips Like the Ones You Are Reading Now!

Since Boyer (1990) redefined scholarship, there have been many definitions of SoTL (Kern, Mettetal, Dixson, & Morgan, 2015). According to Hutchings and Shulman (1999), SoTL is distinguished by inquiry that is systematic or methodical, shared in order to advance the goals of improving teaching, and that the ultimate goal is to improve students' learning. Given these defining characteristics, you may be led to believe that you must create a methodologically sophisticated research study to become involved in the SoTL arena. Nothing could be further from the truth. While there is SoTL information available (journals, books, etc), it is not always easily transferrable to your classroom. Sometimes applying content that is theoretical or found in an empirical article to the classroom is difficult.

The SoTL community is a warm and welcoming world filled with phenomenal teachers. As such, most began their journey into SoTL by sharing teaching tips with one another. We (the authors) have benefited greatly from teaching tips. Having, someone more advanced than we being willing to say what works and what doesn't work has impacted us professionally and the students with whom we work. Not only have these teaching tips enhanced the learning experience for students in our courses, but we have also seen how valuable these teaching tips are for new faculty. We (the authors) have had the opportunity to train novice instructors in teaching methods and see the benefit of practical teaching advice in improving instruction.

How to Get Started?

- **Think back to your own experiences in teaching.** Every instructor who cares about excellence has found a way to make a particular assignment, activity, feedback method, etc. better for students and/or for themselves. These are the exact ideas that other teachers are searching for. You don't have to publish a study with an experimental design to make a mark in SoTL or to contribute to the field. It may be possible you could impact as many lives publishing a teaching tip as publishing a research a SoTL research article. However, teaching tips make a wonderful starting place for considering a more experimental study of a teaching idea.

- **Consider sharing your teaching tip with others.** A hallmark of scholarship is making one's work public. Locally, consider sharing by presenting your teaching tip at an on-campus workshop, perhaps through the campus center for teaching and learning. Also consider local teaching conferences that frequently allow for presentations that are based on teaching tips. Finally, there are multiple options for publishing these types of teaching tips, including:
    - The *It Works for Me* series you are reading right now.
    - *Quick Hits*: This series, published by Indiana University Press, collects techniques and tips from award winning teachers. The Indiana University Faculty Academy on Excellence in Teaching (FACET) calls for submissions for each new volume published. Currently, there is an ongoing call for teaching tips related to using the learning management system, Canvas.
    - There are also several journals that accept teaching tips. Be sure to check your discipline-based teaching journal as well as general teaching journals.
- **So, what makes a good teaching tip?** First and foremost, the teaching tip must fully describe the instructional approach or innovation so that another person can apply it. This process sounds easy but is harder than it sounds. As faculty, we're accustomed to writing theory; writing a 'how to' may feel awkward. When writing your description, think about including your learning outcomes, tools involved, implementation steps, and a timeline for implementation. It's also useful to state your audience – small class, large class, recitation, lab, clinical, etc. Finally, suggest possible future directions or modifications. Are references necessary? It's nice when a teaching tip is contextualized within the broader scholarly work but not always necessary. Typically, shorter teaching tips lack references while longer ones tend to include them. It's best to review submission guidelines to know whether references are expected.

References

Boyer, E. (1990). *Scholarship reconsidered: Priorities of the professoriate.* Princeton, NJ: Carnegie Foundation for the Advancement of Teaching.

Hutchings, P., & Shulman, L. (1999). The scholarship of teaching new elaborations, new developments. *Change, 31*(5), 11-15.

Kern, B., Mettetal, G., Dixson, M. D., & Morgan, R. K. (2015). The role of SoTL in the academy: Upon the 25th anniversary of Boyer's *Scholarship Reconsidered. Journal of the Scholarship for Teaching and Learning, 15*(3), 1-14. doi: 10.14434/josotl.v15i3.13623

Robin K. Morgan, Indiana University Southeast
Nate Mitchell, Spalding University

SOTL-based Best Practices for Creating Welcoming Classrooms for Students of Color

In the past fifty years, our classrooms have undergone dramatic demographic changes. In 1968, 80% of all college students were white (Rivkin, 2016). By 2012, white students made up only 51% of college students, a percentage which continues to trend downward. Because of these trends, the Scholarship of Teaching and Learning has evolved as well. This article will summarize best practices suggested by the SOTL literature to create classrooms that our welcoming to students of diverse backgrounds.

The first step in creating more welcoming classrooms is to recognize that our current classroom environments are often invalidating to students of color. For example, 63% of students of color reported regularly experiencing microaggressions in academic settings (Boysen et al., 2009). Racial microaggressions, defined as "subtle insults (verbal, nonverbal, and/or visual) directed toward people of color, often automatically or unconsciously," are being committed on a daily basis, both in academic and social aspects of learning environments (Solórzano, Ceja, Yosso, 2000, p. 60). In addition, 44% of students of color report experiencing more overt racist behaviors in their classrooms, from both their colleagues and professors (Boysen et al., 2009). The cumulative effect of these microaggressions and overt racist behaviors is decreased student engagement and academic performance (Boysen et al., 2009).

To combat these problems, Derald Wing Sue, an expert in multicultural issues, suggests having meaningful classroom dialogues to help bridge racial and ethnic divides (Sue, 2015). Self-reflective discussions about race with students are one of the most effective tools to help create a path to mutual respect and understanding. To be productive, these conversations are often difficult because we must recognize, and admit, our own biases and how we are products of cultural conditioning. Authentic conversations require directly dealing with student and professor guardedness that results from denying and minimizing the effects of racism, sexism, and other biases. The key is to have the vulnerability to model honesty, even in admitting our own biases, so that conversations about race do not become stilted and ineffective (Sue, 2015).

A third important research-based recommendation is to understand the classroom from students' perspectives. For example, Stoces, Masner, and Jarolimek (2015) suggest asking all students, but especially socially disadvantaged ones, to identify their preferred ways to learn the material and to try to accommodate them whenever possible. A parallel recommendation is to routinely gather feedback from students to determine what pedagogical interventions, assessment measures, and classroom activities, work well and which do not. Collecting such feedback and fine tuning how you teach in response to it help professors avoid teaching to the dominant social class (Allen, Scott, & Lewis, 2013).

In closing, based on a brief summary of the research cited below, educators should ask themselves the following SOTL-based questions:

- What are my racial biases? Where and how did I develop these beliefs? Am I willing to challenge them?
- What privileges do I have that may inhibit my ability to understand perspectives of students from a minority group?
- Where does my comfort level exist in discussing the topics of race and individuals' experiences of microaggressions, prejudices, and racism, with students?
- How can I facilitate a fair, open, and honest conversation? How can I tell if the conversation becomes unproductive?
- Am I aware of students' perception of the climate of classroom learning and instruction? If so, am I in need of making changes or adjustments?
- Am I aware of how all of my students feel they learn best? Do I provide a fair amount of ways to learn that reaches all of my students?

References

Allen, A., Scott, L. M., & Lewis, C. W. (2013). Racial microaggressions and African American and Hispanic students in urban schools: A call for culturally affirming education. *Interdisciplinary Journal of Teaching and Learning, 3,* 117-129. Retrieved from http://www3.subr.edu/coeijtl/files/Download/IJTL-V3-N2-Summer%202013-Allen-Scott-Lewis-pp117-129.pdf

Boysen, G. A. (2012). Teacher and student perceptions of microaggressions in college classrooms. *College Teaching, 60,* 122-129. doi: 10.1080/87567555.2012.654831.

Rivkin, S. (2016). Desegregation since the Coleman Report. *EducationNext, 16* (2).

Solórzano, D., Ceja, M., Yosso, T. (2001). Critical race theory, racial microaggressions, and campus racial climate: The experiences of African American college students. *Journal of Negro Education, 69,* 60-73. Retrieved from http://advance.uci.edu/ADVANCE%20PDFs/Climate/CRT_RacialMicros_Campus.pdf

Stoces, M., Masner, J., & Jarolimek, J. (2015). Mitigation of social exclusion in regions and rural areas: E-learning with focus on content creation and evaluation. *Agris on-line Papers in Economics and Informatics, 7,* 143-150. Retrieved from http://purl.umn.edu/231943

Sue, D.W. (2015). *Race talk and the conspiracy of silence.* Hoboken, NJ: Wiley.

Mackenzie Hoffman, Spalding University
Michael Daniel, Spalding University
Jimmy Joseph, Spalding University
DeDe Wohlfarth, Spalding University

Fostering an Environment of Discovery through Discussion

Positive student outcomes can be achieved in a myriad of ways. One technique that has proven effective in my classrooms has been to encourage sharing ideas by means of free discussion that is directed loosely. At the beginning of a course let it be known that any addition to the course is welcome and that speaking related thoughts helps everybody. We can apply one of the tenants of the creative discipline by making sure that there is no such thing as a bad or seemingly foolish statement.

In order for this process to be more effective, it is important to provide an environment where students feel comfortable speaking in front of others. Toward this purpose I have found that it is a good idea to arrive early to class and engage the students in conversation about things going on in their lives or events happening locally, nationally, or even internationally. I call this the "coffee shop" method. By making small talk like you would with someone you were seated near in a coffee shop, you make students feel as if they are in a comfortable setting, somewhere where they feel comfortable speaking what comes to mind instead of only thinking it without verbalization.

Very early in a semester I like to have an assignment that puts a small group of students in front of the class to present their own discussion. By doing so, students learn how to direct a discussion and are exposed to how I react in a discussion when I'm not the lead. This technique reinforces to them what I desire from them in a discussion setting.

If we look at instruction by numbers, we find that having one instructor and twenty students mathematically means that each student receives five percent of the instructor. By fostering participation on the part of the student in order to become an active learner, you can transform the students into instructors. Under the direction of the actual instructor the students are capable of helping each other learn, or, in other words, the students become instructors and the ratio of twenty to one becomes one to one. As an aside, I have learned a lot over the years from my students.

To sum up:
- Well planned discussion leads to active learning
- A comfortable setting is important in fostering discussion participation
- Active learning is effective for retention.

Brian Fardo, Eastern Kentucky University

V. Putting Theory Into Practice: An Overview

One of the hallmarks of our *It Works for Me* series is the depth and breadth of actual strategies for implementing the content area (e.g., collaboration, creativity, metacognition) in the teaching-learning experience. That is, we've always believed theories are just that without practical application. Our readers have consistently applauded the user-friendly nature of the collections, employing some tips *in toto* while reshaping others for their individual situations.

In this section you will find the results of melding theory and methodology to produce actual scholarly projects, groups, and activities—all designed to enhance teacher effectiveness and deepen student learning. Whether the tip touches on developing interdisciplinary SOTL collaborations for peer observation, syllabus critique, or classroom teaching; providing more comprehensive feedback for students; assessing effectiveness of classroom strategies; designing projects for real-world application of SOTL principles; or introducing technology into the SOTL arena, each one reveals a unique, practical embodiment of those theories and methodologies covered in earlier sections.

Designing a SoTL Professional Learning Community (PLC) Experience for Faculty Development

The Professional Learning Community (PLC) is a common faculty development initiative across higher education campuses. Although PLCs vary from institution to institution, they often offer a sustained, ongoing effort to provide learning opportunities focused on a broadly applicable topic of interest across disciplines.

The tips contained here will give you plenty to consider as you design a SoTL PLC experience for faculty on your campus.

Potential Weekly Topics

- Defining SoTL on your campus
- Reflecting on SoTL
- Steps in the SoTL process
- Conducting SoTL research and identifying the best method
- Collecting SoTL data
- Confronting challenges often encountered in SoTL projects.

Tips for Designing SoTL-Focused PLCs

SoTL is a major topic across research and teaching-intensive campuses. The following tips can be applied and adapted to fit the needs and expectations at your institution:

- Keep your PLC small if at all possible to ensure time for discussion and questions
- Begin thinking about SoTL research projects from the beginning
- Set goals for each PLC meeting and monitor those goals as they evolve during the experience.

In addition, connect your SoTL PLC plans with existing events and initiatives on campus:

- On-campus conferences focused on teaching and learning

- Undergraduate and graduate showcase events
- Connect faculty with grant support and funding to further their research
- Invite participants to become future leaders or facilitators.

Recommended SoTL Resources for Your PLC

- Bishop-Clark, Cathy, and Beth Dietz-Uhler. (2012). *Engaging in the scholarship of teaching and learning: A guide to the process, and how to develop a project from start to finish.* Sterling, VA: Stylus.
- Hutchins, Pat, Taylor, Mary Buber, and Anthony Ciccone. (2011). *Scholarship of teaching and learning reconsidered: Institutional integration and impact.* San Francisco: Jossey-Bass.
- Savory, Paul, Amy Nelson Burnett, and Amy Goodburn. (2007). *Inquiry into the college Classroom: A journey toward scholarly teaching.* Boston, MA: Anker.

Rusty Carpenter, Eastern Kentucky University
Shirley O'Brien, Eastern Kentucky University

Getting Engaged in a SoTL Community: *Project Syllabus* as an Example from Psychology

In business, many have said "networking is everything." Traditionally, faculty have 'networked' through discipline-based research collaborations and by serving together on committees. Fewer opportunities exist for faculty to 'network' about teaching and even fewer for collaboration regarding SoTL.

Our Definition of a SoTL Community

McKinney (2007) defined the SoTL as going beyond scholarly teaching to the systematic study of teaching and learning, leading to presentations, performance, or publications that allow for public sharing and review. Such work can be completed individually much as discipline-based research can be completed individually. However, we argue that the development of a SoTL community can be advantageous. Such a community might be seen as similar to a faculty learning community that allows faculty to create connections, establish networks, and learn about the SoTL. This group of expert educators would, ideally, be passionate about both high quality teaching and establishing/disseminating empirically supported teaching methods.

Several benefits accrue from getting involved in a SoTL Community:
- Increasing your own knowledge about the literature in disciplinary pedagogy
- Exploring signature pedagogical practice and research methodologies
- Identifying research questions that would enhance approaches to teaching and learning
- Selecting a research problem, designing a methodology, implementing the research, and collecting data
- Surrounding yourself with excellence to stay challenged and excited
- Developing a professional identity in the SoTL field
- Finding a mentor if you are new to the field or profession
- Publishing and presenting SoTL work. Being connected with others within SoTL may allow you to find a niche by filling a need you may not have known was there.
- Identifying leadership opportunities in professional organizations
- Developing new professional opportunities. Being recognized as an expert and leader within SoTL may lead to opportunities to serve as an editor for a teaching journal, increase marketability when considering new academic positions, or create opportunities within faculty development such as directing your campus center for teaching excellence.

Project Syllabus as an Example from Psychology

The Society for the Teaching of Psychology (Division 2 of the American Psychological Association) sponsors Project Syllabus, which reviews and publishes exemplary syllabi. A team of invited reviewers provide blind reviews of submitted syllabi, using a rubric focused on best practices in syllabus design.

Reviewing syllabi requires staying up to date with syllabus research and provides an opportunity to give feedback on improving syllabi to instructors, hopefully improving teaching and learning outcomes. Being a reviewer also allows for thoughtful self-critique of one's own syllabi, based on current standards. In addition to the review process, numerous presentation and publication opportunities for the current reviewers through

Project Syllabus exist. Reviewers are given the opportunity to collaborate on presentations at the annual American Psychological Association conference, the National Institute on the Teaching of Psychology annual conference, and to work on research articles based on Project Syllabus initiatives.

Finally, leadership opportunities and networking opportunities within Division 2, the Society for Teaching of Psychology, are available through Project Syllabus. Reviewers can become the Director of Project Syllabus or seek election to serve in a number of leadership positions within Division 2.

Twenty years ago, few faculty considered SoTL. Even today, many faculty are unaware of the growing literature in SoTL. Such a situation presents unique opportunities. First, a faculty member can develop a niche in this area, quickly becoming a campus authority when it comes to SoTL. Becoming an expert may be most effectively achieved by joining an existing SoTL community, such as Project Syllabus, or by developing a SoTL community, such as a faculty learning community on SoTL. The advantages of such a SoTL learning community can quickly enable a faculty member to develop stronger SoTL projects, connect with others who are interested in SoTL, present and publish within SoTL, and develop as an emerging leader within SoTL.

Reference

McKinney, K. (2007). *Enhancing learning through the scholarship of teaching and learning.* Bolton, MA: Anker.

Nate Mitchell, Spalding University
Robin K. Morgan, Indiana University Southeast
Jonathan W. Carrier, Laramie County Community College

Transdisciplinary Faculty and Graduate Student Collaboration to Train our Future Teachers and Researchers: the Bailey Scholars Method

Higher education is seeking ways to prepare future faculty members to unite the worlds of teaching and research. Existing methods include the use of exchanges among university branches, mentorship and co-teaching in experiential classrooms, and faculty and student development workshops (Walters and Misra, 2013; Jauregui, 2013). The Bailey Scholars Program (BSP) at Michigan State University provides graduate students with a one-year, intensive fellowship to explore new teaching methods, practice research, and publish with diverse authors.

BSP uses a Montessori-based approach to help undergraduate students learn how they learn and foster cognitive connections among their major, their electives, and their passions. The classroom promotes diversity of epistemological views as the undergraduate students, graduate fellows, and faculty unite from across the University. Furthermore, the Montessori approach promotes equality, allowing the students and conveners (the title used by fellows while in the classroom) to collaborate in building the course syllabus. In this fashion, the graduate students learn how to effectively deliver a course and meet learning goals while doing so in a method rare in higher education.

Beginning in 2010, BSP offered their Graduate Fellows the opportunity to link their passions in both research and teaching by convening in a BSP classroom and engaging in a SoTL research project. While each fellow works with individual faculty in the classroom, the six fellows and the BSP Director meet as a team at orientation to outline their goals and design their own research project. To date, these have included the transformative impacts study abroad as well as coding student learning reflections for incidental learning characteristics. The fellows continue to foster the connections between research and teaching in attending and presenting their work at conferences and moving the research into peer-reviewed articles.

A key tip for success is the diversity of the graduate fellows. The applicants do not need an education-based background or major. Past fellows have represented majors as varied as construction management, criminal justice, fisheries and wildlife, psychology, and statistics. The diverse teammates bring different literature to explore, methods to practice, and world-views to understand the research findings. Each fellow can bring the knowledge gained through this unique classroom and research experience to their own department.

In addition to monthly meetings to track progress of the research, BSP offers a potluck dinner called "Core Course Share Night." Here, the undergraduate students present to the BSP community their learning outcomes and the methods uses to achieve their goals. In attending, the fellows are able to see the differences among the 200, 300, and 400 level students and explore different means to achieve learning.

Each year, the fellows and the undergraduate students vary. While the fellows provide diversity of means, the ends must be successful with each process. It is vital to success that the faculty, including the BSP Director, maintains a consistent vision to align individual courses and each research project to the University's vision and needs. The faculty's role in ensuring the "big picture" goals can be achieved further permits the fellows to experiment with and explore alternative methods.

Many of the past fellows have since completed their PhDs and continue research and teaching in their respective fields. These graduates often did not have classroom experience outside of this fellowship. As faculty today have increasing demands in both their research and teaching, the BSP fellowship experience offers one means to establish a collaborative relationship among faculty and students and better train graduate students seeking jobs in higher education.

References

Jauregui, M. (2013). *Cross-cultural training of expatriate faculty teaching in international branch campuses.* (Doctoral dissertation). University of Southern California, Los Angeles.

Walters, K., & Misra, J. (2013). Bringing Collaborative Teaching into Doctoral Programs: Faculty and Graduate Student Co-teaching as Experiential Training. *The American Sociologist, 44*(3), 292-301.

Robert Dalton, Michigan State University
Pat Crawford, Michigan State University

Lesson Study: A Means for Faculty Collaboration

Lesson study is an intensive professional development activity used in Japan to improve instruction in K-12 schools (Stepanek et al. 2007, p.2). It has been adapted for use in post-secondary settings. Lesson study requires teachers to move beyond their unconscious expectations for teaching to examining each stage of the process. Lesson study provides a framework for thinking deeply about teaching by working collaboratively to investigate new approaches to teaching. As such, it provides an excellent means for modeling collaborative SoTL research. It can be a useful technique in helping junior faculty understand the SoTL process. This essay will examine how we implemented a cross-disciplinary lesson study faculty development seminar at our institution.

Lesson study teams begin by collaboratively developing a lesson. This lesson differs dramatically from traditional lessons. In traditional lessons the focus is guided by content, and lessons are frequently teacher-centered and course specific. However, in a lesson study lesson, the focus is on uncovering material. This approach is student-centered and oriented to evaluating student learning as a result of the lesson. Faculty spend time together exploring their own experiences, ideas they have heard, and researching the literature on the concept or procedure to be taught. As faculty engage in this collaborative exercise, they take into account their students' prior knowledge and how students learn.

In our seminar, we ask participating faculty to consider their long-term goals focused on what students will be able to do or know in the future after completing the course. We encourage participating instructors to think about what students should know or be able to do five years later? What should students be able to know or do with that information? This kind of long-term view with broad parameters helps participants envision the place of their course within a student's program of study. It also provides insight into how the lesson fits within the course curriculum. Once the team has thought through the course, they are able to use the long-term vision to identify short-term goals for students to complete during the course.

The faculty team identifies the unit the learning goals fit within. They develop unit-specific goals that help connect the long-term course goal to specific lesson goals. The unit goals identify the most appropriate place in the curriculum to insert the lesson. For example, here is a goal written by a lesson study team of faculty from journalism, English, and communication:

Our goal was to develop students who critically, skeptically and thoroughly evaluate sources and articulate the benefits of spending time on this kind of activity. We want students to be able to apply what they learned from this lesson more broadly in their major discipline and in their pursuit of knowledge beyond college. We want students to be able to critically think about and evaluate the credibility of information that they gather in future research endeavors. The value of this lesson crosses many disciplines and has applications beyond the classroom.

Once the team identifies the goal, they think through what ideal students would be able to do in their course and in the lesson. Then they examine what students are actually able to do in their course and in the lesson. The instructors work to identify the student qualities that will be developed in the lesson. They discuss how students might react to the lesson by considering questions such as "What do students already know about the concept?" and "What points of the lesson will students have difficulty with?" Once instructors have thought through possible student reactions, they examine what they can do to make the lesson at the appropriate level for students so that it is challenging without being overwhelming or too easy. Then, the team identifies possible instructional activities, key concepts students will explore, and considers how they will scaffold learning for all students. Finally, the instructors must address assessment of student learning. Instructors consider the question, "How will we know our students have learned?" They think about what evidence they might use to show student learning and how they can use that evidence to improve student learning.

Once the lesson is ready, a volunteer team member teaches the lesson and the others observe and debrief, which involves analyzing the evidence they collected of student learning. The team then begins work on revising the lesson, re-teaching it, and then another debriefing. The team finally reflects on the lesson and shares results with others.

We asked the faculty team to follow a three part report for sharing their lesson study work. In the background section, we asked the lesson study teams to identify the courses in which the lesson was taught along with course descriptions. They also describe the lesson's learning goals, plan, and major findings. In the second section, the teams describe the lesson plan in detail so others can implement it. They are asked to provide timings of activities, explanations for activities, and any areas where students might have difficulty. In the final section, they report their SoTL results as findings.

Lesson study is an excellent way to support initial SoTL projects. Cerbin (2011) argues "because it embodies all five elements of teaching—vision, design, interactions, outcomes, and analysis—lesson study is an ideal context in which to document teaching improvement" (116). Lesson study facilitates examining the relationships between the instructor's goals for student learning, the design of the lessons, the interactions in the classroom, the changes in student learning, and the analysis of student learning that can be used to document effective teaching. Faculty in our seminars found lesson study an effective means of examining their own teaching and for documenting their work as teachers.

References

Cerbin, B. (2011). *Lesson study: Using classroom inquiry to improve teaching and learning in higher education.* Sterling, VA: Stylus.

Stepanek, J., Appel, G., Leong, M., Turner-Mangan, M, & Mitchell, M. (2007). *Leading lesson study: A practical guide for teachers and facilitators.* Thousand Oaks, CA: Corwin Press.

Brenda Refaei, University of Cincinnati Blue Ash College
Rita Kumar, University of Cincinnati Blue Ash College

Interdepartmental Faculty Collaboration

Adam and Mary Lou, faculty members at the same university, met during a professional development opportunity for teaching in interactive learning spaces, classrooms with flexible seating and enhanced technology to support pedagogy (e.g., Vercellotti, *forthcoming*). When Adam won the Excellence in Teaching Award, he decided to incorporate authentic Spanish language materials into his beginning-level Spanish course. Authentic materials include texts and videos created for a native speaker audience rather than targeted towards learners of the language (Harwood, 2010). When Mary Lou heard his plan to make this change to his already excellent teaching, she encouraged him to document the process and to write about it as SoTL. Adam was hesitant. Adam was concerned about the time and effort needed to complete the SoTL project while enacting the pedagogical change. Mary Lou offered to manage the researcher tasks so that Adam could focus on the instructor tasks (finding materials and creating assignments) during the semester of data collection. A SoTL collaboration was born.

We searched for published work on the topic and shared the articles and our opinions about them. After our literature review, it was clear that this SoTL project would be valuable to other language teachers who want to know how to best incorporate authentic materials into courses. Recognizing the importance of sharing the SoTL project with the field really motivated us to collaborate so that the work could be published.

Adam wanted to include his students' opinions about their perceptions and experiences of the pedagogical change. Adam drafted questions in a Google Form survey; Mary Lou gave feedback on questions and the wording. Together, we finalized the questions and the format of the survey. For instance, should the survey allow the students to choose more than one response? In order to include the students' perspectives with a larger audience (via academic presentations or publications), the research required approval from the Institutional Review Board (IRB) and informed consent from the students. Mary Lou completed and submitted the IRB paperwork. To avoid any appearance of coercion or risk of grade bias, instructors cannot ask their own students to participate in research, so Mary Lou served in the researcher role in Adam's class. At the end of the semester, after the submission of grades, we looked at the anonymous survey responses about the students' perceptions of the use of authentic materials and looked for themes in the students' responses. It was also interesting to see the change in student perceptions and responses across the semester as the students grew more confident in their content (Spanish) knowledge and more comfortable with employing various language comprehension strategies to comprehend the "real-world" authentic materials.

Throughout the semester, Adam wrote reflections about what he did and how he, as an instructor, perceived the success of and the ease of completing each activity and/or assignment with authentic materials. Adam shared his reflections with Mary Lou during the semester, and we met to discuss the process of incorporating these materials and to gauge the success of its implementation. It is often useful to have a person to talk with, to ask critical questions, especially when turning that experience into SoTL research. Mary Lou asked Adam open-ended questions in semi-structured retrospective interviews (Loughran, 2002) about the process of making pedagogical change and any noticeable effects on the students learning. For instance, Mary Lou asked how the changes were related to the learning objectives and how Adam could gauge the effectiveness of the assignments. The time to exchange ideas was inspiring for both of us.

The next semesters, we met to plan, write, and submit our SoTL findings. First, we reviewed our research questions and identified which could be crafted into a coherent article for a specific audience. A search of relevant journals revealed a call for articles on our specific topic, the use of authentic materials in language classrooms, which exactly matched our main research question. Other manuscripts are possible because the data were so rich.

During our collaboration meetings, we have discussed more than this SoTL research; we have also shared teaching tips and ideas for using pedagogical technology. And, we have chatted about life. It has been validating and motivating for our professional growth to connect with someone from a different department within the same university, someone who can be an unbiased, supportive ear about teaching, course development, and balancing teaching and research.

Instructors often introduce a new pedagogical practice. We almost reflectively evaluate its effectiveness and what can be further revised to improve our courses, but often this process is informal and maybe incomplete. As part of a SoTL project, the teaching effectiveness evaluation is fleshed-out beyond a personal reflection. By making the reflections explicit to another person, we gain more insight about the process as we are challenged to verbalize our informal evaluations and assumptions. This collaboration provided a multi-dimensional view of the SoTL process, including student-to-researcher survey data, teacher-to-self reflection data, and teacher-to-researcher interviews and discussion data. The interdepartmental faculty collaboration has made a bigger impact on our teaching, and it has led to more robust SoTL research to be shared with the field.

References

Harwood, N. (2010). *English language teaching materials: Theory and practice.* Cambridge, MA: Cambridge Language Education.

Loughran, J. J. (2002). Effective reflective practice: In search of meaning in learning about teaching. *Journal of Teacher Education, 53*(1), 33-43.

Vercellotti, M. L. (*forthcoming*). Do interactive learning spaces increase student achievement? A comparison of classroom context. *Active Learning in Higher Education.*

Adam Ballart, Ball State University
Mary Lou Vercellotti, Ball State University

Interdisciplinary Peer Observation Groups

Professional development in college teaching is frequently focused on specific content areas and often misses innovative teaching strategies utilized in other academic fields. For example, a conference on best practices in teaching psychology may cover a range of effective approaches for teaching within the field of psychology, but may not examine cutting edge classroom practices that may be present within such fields as English, Mathematics, or History. Additionally, conference attendance for professional development in college teaching can be costly and sometimes lack in meaningful collaboration between faculty members.

It can be easy for faculty to forget that innovative and highly effective teaching strategies are being employed around them every day at the institutions in which they teach. In order to tap this in-house teaching expertise, faculty can form interdisciplinary peer observation groups. In these peer observation groups, faculty members from different academic areas observe their peers teaching a class session, followed by a group discussion of the effective teaching strategies observed. The observation groups conclude with a discussion of how faculty members can adapt the observed teaching strategies for use in their own classes.

An interdisciplinary peer observation group could be implemented in the following manner: Six faculty members representing the six unique academic areas of Psychology, History, Statistics, English, Literature, and Mathematics agree to observe each other's classes. These six faculty members form two subgroups of three faculty members, in which each faculty member is observed by two other faculty members. It should be noted that subgroups are necessary for larger groups of participating faculty members because having more than two faculty members observing a classroom session may be unnerving to the students and/or the faculty member being observed.

In this example, Subgroup 1 might be comprised of an English instructor, a History instructor, and a Mathematics instructor. In Subgroup 1, a class session taught by the English instructor would be observed by the History instructor and the Mathematics instructor. The History instructor would then be observed by the English Instructor and the Mathematics instructor. Finally, the Mathematics instructor would be observed by the English instructor and the History instructor.

Subgroup 2 would be comprised of a Psychology instructor, a Statistics instructor, and a Literature instructor. In Subgroup 2, a class session taught by the Psychology instructor would be observed by the Statistics instructor and the Literature instructor. Next, the Statistics instructor would be observed by the Psychology instructor and the Literature instructor. Finally, the Literature instructor would be observed by the Statistics instructor and the Psychology instructor.

At this point in the process, all six faculty members reconvene as a main group and take turns presenting the most effective teaching strategies they saw during their subgroup classroom observations. Because not all of the six participating faculty members observed every class taught by the other participating faculty members, this step allows every faculty member to be exposed to all other participating faculty members' most effective strategies. As an example, in Subgroup 1, the Mathematics instructor may discuss the English instructor's effective use of group work. In Subgroup 2, the Statistics instructor may discuss how impressed he/she was with the Literature instructor's use of participative learning.

Finally, all six faculty members reconvene as a main group again to discuss how participating instructors plan to apply the effective teaching strategies they saw in the other faculty members' classes to their own classes. For example, the Mathematics instructor may detail how he plans to adopt similar group work strategies to what he observed in the English instructor's class. Similarly, the Statistics instructor may describe her plans to encourage the same type of participative learning that she observed in the Literature instructor's class.

In sum, interdisciplinary peer observation groups offer college faculty the ability to not only showcase the most effective teaching strategies in their disciplines, but also to learn effective strategies from faculty in other academic areas that can then be adapted to teaching in their own disciplines. Faculty who regularly engage in interdisciplinary peer observation groups have unending opportunities for professional development within their home institutions.

Steps to implementing an Interdisciplinary Peer Observation Group:
- Step 1: Form a group of faculty from unique academic areas
- Step 2: If the participating faculty group is large, divide the group into two or more subgroups
- Step 3: Have each member of the group/subgroup observe one class session taught by the other members of the group/subgroup
- Step 4: Reconvene the main group of participating faculty and present the most effective teaching strategies observed in the other faculty members' class sessions
- Step 5: Reconvene the main group of participating faculty a final time and discuss how faculty members intend to incorporate the effective teaching strategies they observed in other faculty members' classes into their own teaching.

Jonathan W. Carrier, Laramie County Community College
Nate Mitchell, Spalding University

Evaluating the Long-Term Impact of Practicum Courses on Students

Instructors in higher education across many disciplines offer practicum courses to give students experience in professions they may pursue after graduation (Garris, Madden, & Rodgers, 2008; Krasynska, Jones, & Schumann, 2013, Villanueva, Hovinga, & Cass, 2011). The courses are designed to help students understand the work involved in these professions and enhance their ability to undertake it. The Stanford Public Policy

Program offers a practicum course, in which undergraduate and graduate students work in small teams to conduct program evaluations and policy analyses for nonprofits and government agencies. We designed the course to help students improve various policy analysis skills and general professional skills that we expected would be useful in a variety of professions.

After offering the practicum course for five years, our program wanted to determine if the course's objectives were being met. Although students favorably reviewed the course in their course evaluations, we needed feedback from former students who could tell us whether they found their practicum experience useful after graduation. We also wanted to know if the course affected their career paths and interests. If the course was not achieving its objectives, we wanted to find out how it could be redesigned to better achieve them.

To obtain this feedback, a colleague and I conducted a survey of all students who had taken the course during its first five years. The 26-question online survey consisted of both closed-ended and free response questions addressing the student's practicum experience and its impact after the course ended. With an introductory email and two reminders, we obtained an 82% response rate.

For quantifying the course's impact on skills, we asked students to use a 5-point Likert scale to rate their improvement in nine skills due to the practicum, and then rate the usefulness of each skill after graduation. The skills included applying policy analysis skills to address a real problem, writing for a policy audience, research design, collecting and preparing data for analysis, quantitative methods, team management, project management, oral presentation skills, and communication with clients and other professionals.

To gauge the practicum's impact on career paths and interests, students rated how interested they were before and after the practicum in public service and in jobs that included policy analysis work. They indicated whether they used their practicum experience in one or more specific ways in their job search and/or graduate school applications (e.g., discussed in interview). They were also asked to describe with as much detail as possible how the course influenced their work in a professional or academic context after graduation. In addition, we included a question about how useful the practicum had been to them overall.

To help us improve or redesign the course, we asked students to rate how much of a barrier 11 factors presented for undertaking their practicum project, such as project scope, data availability, client accessibility, and time constraints. We inquired about how useful six course-related resources were (e.g., the campus' writing center and oral communication program). We also asked whether they should have received additional training before conducting their project and what suggestions they had for improving the course.

We learned a substantial amount from these and other survey questions. The results indicated that the course was accomplishing its objective of helping students improve policy analysis skills and general professional skills that were useful in their professional lives. From the students' open-ended responses, we learned that the practicum experience was valuable in a variety of positions, including policy analyst, management consultant, paralegal, educator, investment banker, and venture capitalist. The practicum had increased student interest in policy analysis jobs and public service. In addition, half of the students had listed their practicum project on their resume and even more had discussed it in an interview.

From the survey results, our program decided to retain the practicum course's basic structure and to continue to require it as the capstone course for all Master in Public Policy students and for undergraduates majoring in Public Policy who were not writing honors theses. However, the students' feedback led us to make several changes to the course. For example, to better prepare students for their practicum experience, instructors began offering more training in applied quantitative methods before students began their course projects.

The survey results have been used in other ways as well. Program faculty and staff have referenced our study to help sell the practicum course and program to prospective students, potential practicum instructors and client organizations, and the university administration. We published our study in the *Journal of Public Affairs Education* (Sprague & Percy, 2014), adding to the literature on the impact of practicum experiences on students. On our program website, we have a link to the article so students, faculty, and others are able to learn more about the course and its impact.

Based on this experience, I encourage practicum instructors and administrators to survey their former students to help determine whether their courses are having their intended long-term impact and to assess how their courses might need to change to better achieve their objectives. In surveying the students, I recommend including some students who have graduated at least a few years earlier as they have had more time to observe the course's impact on their professional lives. The survey would also benefit from both closed-ended and free response questions, because the former help quantify the course's impact and the latter reveal unanticipated information and help researchers better understand the numerical results.

References

Garris, R., Madden, J., & Rodgers, W. M., III. (2008). Practitioners' roles, internships, and practicum courses in public policy and management education. *Journal of Policy Analysis and Management, 27*(4), 992–1003.

Krasynska, S., Jones, J. A., & Schumann, M. J. (2013). *Applied projects evaluation: Organizational impact report.* San Diego, CA: University of San Diego School of Leadership and Education Sciences. Retrieved from https://lib.sandiego.edu/soles/ documents/Applied%20ProjectsReport83113.pdf

Sprague, M., & Percy, R. C. (2014). The immediate and long-term impact of practicum experiences on students. *Journal of Public Affairs Education, 20*(1), 91–111.

Villanueva, A. M., Hovinga, M. E., & Cass, J. L. (2011). Master of public health community-based practicum: Students' and preceptors' experiences. *Journal of Public Health Management and Practice, 17*(4), 337–343.

Mary Sprague, Stanford University

SoTL Works for Doctoral Students in Education

The doctoral program in Educational Leadership at Eastern Kentucky University uses the Scholarship of Teaching and Learning (SoTL) as one model for preparing dissertations. As a professor in the doctoral program, I [Bill] work directly with students who are interested in developing a research topic that uses SoTL as the format. The students begin with research and policy classes and then define and refine a research topic with a field experience course. During this field experience, the student must state a topic, conduct a review of literature on the topic, and spend thirty hours with an expert on the topic to refine the statement of the problem. A second field experience is required to further refine the topic and the statement of the problem. So two semesters are spent doing field experiences, reviewing the literature, and defining and refining the topic. Because they have had time to reflect with a practitioner who is an expert in the field, often their methodology lends itself to SoTL.

The doctoral program was designed as a practical doctorate with a field experience that has become an integral part of the clinical model. Therefore, the dissertation flows out of the field experience and often lends itself to SoTL. As a dissertation chair, I work with students to further refine the statement of the problem and research questions that are important to the topic and aligned with SoTL. The following is an example of one student's dissertation that is currently in process and a report he wrote for me about how his field experience led her to a SoTL model.

According to Jamie:

> My dissertation will be a longitudinal study of Somerset Community College developmental mathematics graduation/credential rates from 1998 to 2016 where I will analyze data to determine if any trends or improvements exist in the graduation rate, given the developmental mathematics interventions implemented during the longitudinal time span.

As I [Jamie] met with my mentors, each experience yielded more questions about why students graduate high schools and are not college ready. These questions have led me to stratify my dissertation study sample to focus on developmental mathematics students from Wayne County: (1) Were there any support mechanisms in place at the college that might have supported or hindered improvement in developmental mathematics student graduation rates? (2) What math curriculum changes, if any, occurred at the high school prior to enrolling at SCC that might explain the changes in college developmental mathematics student performance? (3) What student support mechanisms were in place in high school that would foster improved student engagement? And, (4) Given that eleventh grade students are tested, what mechanisms have been in place to provide assistance to non-college ready twelfth grade students the following year?

I have begun to frame questions around our discussions and around my new experiences in the high school mathematics classroom. One of the most frustrating changes is the focus around the use of the technology to solve problems, as opposed to algebra. Below is the dialogue of a conversation about a math lesson that I recently had with a student in an Algebra II class:

> Me: I have a question for you, class. How can I analyze a quadratic?
> Student: Ms. Foster, should we answer in Converge, using our calculators, with Plickers, or do you want a paper answer?
> Me: I just want a verbal answer to the question. Tell me something about the quadratic using math vocabulary.
> Student: We don't do that in any other class; we do everything using technology!

This conversation caused me to ponder about how I, as a mathematician, can justify this focus on the use of the graphing calculator to solve problems to the detriment of learning how to think critically and obtain solutions by analysis and algebraic problem solving.

I shared this conversation with all three of my mentors, and they all unanimously agreed that standardized testing and the pressure on students to become college ready on the ACT, which is part of the Kentucky system of accountability for K-12 schools, are likely the culprit.

During one meeting, I asked one mentor to explain his newly designed initiative, Cardinal University. He shared that this initiative would enable high school students who desired to complete an associate degree, to do so before graduating high school. He explained that the data he obtained from analyzing ACT scores and dual credit participation led him to work with EKU, WKU, SCC, and Campbellsville University to expand the dual credit offering to include some online courses from each of the four institutions. This partnership, in conjunction with scholarships provided by KHEAA through the Governor's new high school initiative, enabled students to attain credit hours without resulting in huge financial burdens to families.

My experience with doctoral students has taught me that SoTL is a valuable tool.

Bill Phillips, Eastern Kentucky University
Jamie Foster, Wayne County High School, KY

Projects for Business Students

At our institution, we wanted to give business students an opportunity to add "bullet points" to their resumes beyond just internships or working a semester in the campus library (both valuable experiences, however). But embedded within the classes, we desired to give students concrete, real-world experiences.

To that end, we added a wide variety of projects – for a grade – that not only drove home the material covered in the courses, but also gave the students readily applicable practitioner experience they could showcase on their resumes or in interviews.

It works like this. Faculty contact area businesses, nonprofits, and government entities. This contact usually occurs during the summer months. We ask, "What projects do you have that you don't have the time, staff, or budget to tackle?" Specifically, we are looking for projects that *don't* involve answering phones, filing, and the like. In other words, we seek actual projects that help the organization. We also remind them that these will be college students completing the projects. Therefore, the "clients" should avoid overly complex projects or ones that require specialized knowledge.

Students work in teams of three to five on each project. For the Human Resources Management course, for example, past projects have included designing a performance review form, developing a new hire orientation, conducting a wage survey, and crafting recruitment ads. In marketing research, some past projects have been mystery shopping, conducting focus groups, designing surveys, and doing traffic counts at a busy intersection.

Not only do the students (and clients) enjoy these projects, but the students receive exactly the kinds of experiences potential employers are looking for.

To make the projects as real as possible, students and clients draft a contract detailing what both parties will agree to do. For the client, this obligation is often as simple as saying they will provide the necessary information for students to complete the projects and will answer emails or phone calls in a timely manner. Some clients have students sign non-disclosure agreements if they are dealing with sensitive or proprietary information. For the students' part of the contract, their stipulations are usually that they will accurately and fully complete the project by the deadline.

To ensure students stay on track with their projects, checkpoints throughout the semester give students a chance to share with other students the progress they are making. For example, the first check-point is a presentation about who their client is and the nature of the project. Three weeks later, the students report on how the project is moving along and challenges they may be having. Later checkpoints are workshopping recommendations for the client as well as the final presentation to the client.

Feedback from the last fifteen years has shown that students value these projects immensely and many clients work with our students on a continuing basis, finding new projects every semester. For the faculty, it is quite a logistical feat when starting and making initial contacts with potential clients. After a few semesters, the process becomes much easier as clients who are satisfied with these projects continue to offer new ones regularly. We are now at the point where we often have more projects available than student teams.

Steven Austin Stovall, Wilmington College

Becoming Scholarly Teachers: Assigning a Pedagogical Strategy Paper and Discussion Forum to Teach Doctoral Students About SoTL

We designed and previously co-taught the class *Pedagogy in Health Behavior*, an academic credit-bearing course for doctoral student instructors in the Department of Applied Health Science at Indiana University-Bloomington. Doctoral students with teaching responsibilities are required to enroll in the semester-long course prior to becoming instructors of record or teaching assistants for undergraduate public health courses. Grounded in the scholarship of teaching and learning (SoTL), *Pedagogy in Health Behavior* aims to equip doctoral students with the knowledge to think critically about their teaching practice and to enhance their pedagogical skillset. More information on the overall course and its effectiveness can be found elsewhere (Lederer, Sherwood-Laughlin, Kearns, & O'Loughlin, 2016).

One of the assignments that we developed to help achieve the course goals was a pedagogical strategy paper and accompanying discussion forum. Due at the course mid-point and directly before students begin teaching, this assignment asks students to select a pedagogical strategy that is of interest to them, conduct a literature review, and then consider the utility of the pedagogical tool based on the evidence identified. Students have chosen topics such as: PowerPoint, lecture, humor, cooperative learning, social media, service learning, case studies, interactive response systems, personal testimony, concept mapping, role playing, and story structure. The specific requirements for the written assignment entail having students write a five-page paper (excluding references) with the following headings: background, evidence, synthesis/conclusion, and application. The background section provides a description of the pedagogical strategy, its goals, and what is known about the extent of its use in the college classroom. In the evidence section, at least ten peer-reviewed or other credible sources that have examined the effectiveness of the pedagogical strategy are summarized. For the synthesis/conclusion portion, the main points from the SoTL literature are determined and a conclusion is drawn as to if the evidence supports, supports only under certain circumstances, or rejects the pedagogical strategy's use in the college classroom. In the application section, students are asked to consider how or if they would apply the pedagogical strategy in their own upcoming teaching. When students submit their assignment, they are also instructed to provide a separate summary of just a few sentences about the pedagogical technique, focusing on how it can be best applied, assuming it should be at all. We compiled these synopses into a handout for students as a tangible reminder and future reference about the evidence behind the totality of pedagogical strategies students reviewed for the assignment.

The due date of the pedagogical strategy paper coincides with an in-class pedagogical strategy discussion forum, in which the entirety of the class session is dedicated to having students review their pedagogical strategy and what they learned, having student colleagues pose questions, and engaging in group discussion about each pedagogical strategy's utility. The pedagogical strategy discussion forum provides a valuable medium for students to show their emerging expertise in the SoTL literature on a specific pedagogical topic and to build students' collective SoTL knowledge through the multiple pedagogical tools discussed.

The final assignment for *Pedagogy in Health Behavior* is a course portfolio. Due on the last day of class, the course portfolio is a compendium of revised class assignments. For the pedagogical strategy paper, students are asked to submit their initial paper, but to add a description of their integration (or lack thereof) of the pedagogical strategy in their classroom, including how it was utilized and their perception of its impact, or the rationale for not using the strategy. Most students reported applying their researched pedagogical tool and documented positive experiences doing so. Some students mentioned feeling more confident using the pedagogical strategy after becoming familiar with the evidence behind it. Many doctoral student instructors stated that although they had already planned to use the pedagogical strategy in their teaching, they modified its use based on the best practices they discovered while writing their paper. For example, a 2015 doctoral student instructor who explored PowerPoint for her pedagogical strategy wrote the following: "The pedagogical research paper became a very useful tool as a new instructor. Not only did it give me a deeper insight into what the suggested guidelines are when it comes to the use of PowerPoint, it also helped me to better understand how students perceive its use from perspectives I had not thought of." A few students even became inspired to conduct their own SoTL research studies on the pedagogical strategy they investigated based on gaps they identified in the literature.

The pedagogical strategy paper and discussion forum were valuable for students in a multitude of ways. The assignment synergistically focused on research and teaching, ideal for students enrolled in a PhD program that emphasizes research training but that also provides teaching preparation. The assignment provided an opportunity for students to practice identifying credible sources, thinking critically about literature, synthesizing evidence, and to perform academic writing. It allowed students to showcase their work, demonstrate expertise, have constructive dialogue, and to learn from one another. It portrayed the variety of research methods that can be used in SoTL research and illustrated that teaching can be studied as rigorously as discipline-based research questions. The assignment showed students how to use evidence to inform their teaching and cultivated more scholarly teachers. Ultimately the pedagogical strategy paper and discussion forum exemplified the value of SoTL for novice teachers, which should serve them and their students well throughout their teaching careers.

Reference

Lederer, A. M., Sherwood-Laughlin, C., Kearns, K.D., & O'Loughlin, V.D. (2016). The development and evaluation of a doctoral-level public health pedagogy course for graduate student instructors. *College Teaching, 64*(1), 19-27.

Alyssa M. Lederer, Tulane University
Catherine M. Sherwood-Laughlin, Indiana University-Bloomington

Creating Online Presence: Weekly Video Feedback Brings Everyone Together

Creating online courses as engaging, interactive and empowering has long been a goal of online instructors, course designers, and student learners. Empirical studies repeatedly suggest that building a community of inquiry in online courses is absolutely vital to this end (Garrison, Anderson, & Archer, 2000, 2001; Loureiro-Koechlin & Allan, 2010; Smyth, 2011). A learning community, however, does not develop automatically in any classroom whether online, face-to-face, or blended. Instead, learning communities demand carefully designed teaching and learning environments and must be fostered by all who participate in course development and implementation. Our roles as collaborators in an online course melded content expertise with instructional design. Using the Scholarship of Teaching and Learning (SoTL) process, we evaluated the use of weekly video feedback to enhance online presence, thus promoting meaningful conversations and creating an authentic learning community in an interdisciplinary graduate level online course.

The instructional design strategies and technologies implemented in this course included: 1) Group text-based discussion and blog assignments in Blackboard; 2) Multimedia-based weekly faculty feedback through Adobe Connect videos; and 3) Visual analysis of weekly student interactions. All work was completed asynchronously, within set time parameters for the submission/review of materials.

Due to the nature of the student population in this class (most of whom are full-time professionals), it was inevitable that the text-based asynchronous communication remained as the main interaction method for the students. To increase and enhance the interaction among students, the instructor transformed the class activities from an individual level to a group-level in which students were assigned to interdisciplinary groups. Every student was expected to communicate with group members to create their reflections on weekly synthesis prompts of learning materials (video, readings, etc.) as a team. All individual group discussions were made available for whole class review when the deadline of the assignment expired. This process allowed students an opportunity to review other group's work, enabling them to learn from other groups, much like small groups reporting their work back to the entire class for synthesis.

The instructor's presence is essential for the development of a learning community. In this class, the instructor's presence was carried out through the weekly video feedback. Hattie and Timperley (2007) assert that "Feedback is one of the most powerful

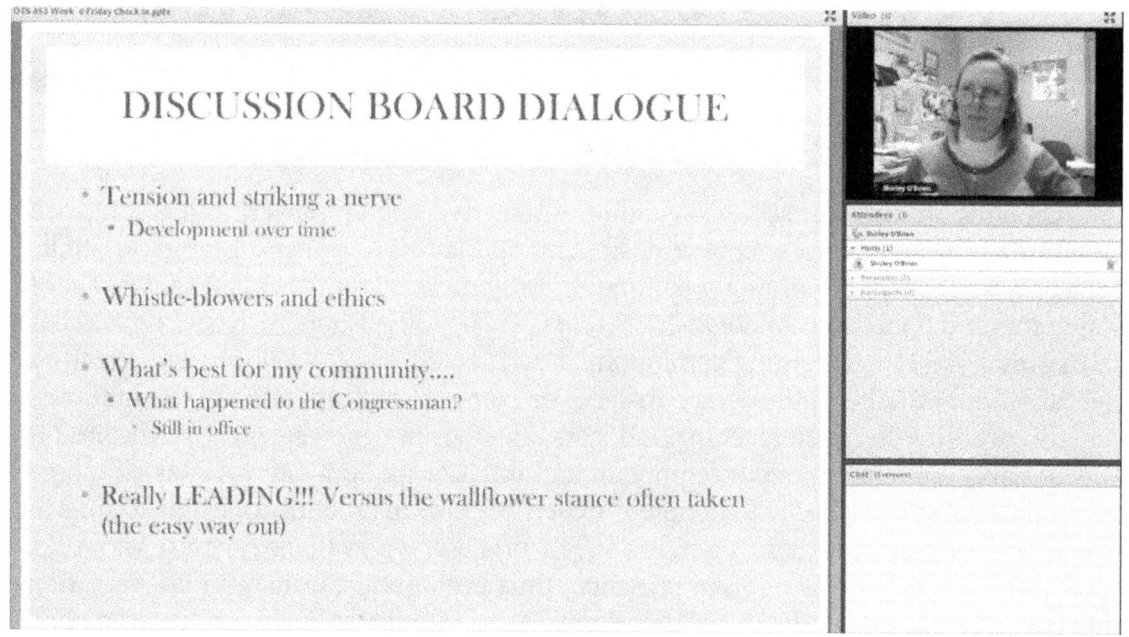

Figure 1: The instructor reviewed the discussion board dialogue in her weekly check-in video.

influences on learning and achievement, but this impact can be either positive or negative" (p. 81). This strategy is effective, reinforcing the learning process of weekly modular applications and how each week added more in-depth content. Following the same principle, the instructor reviewed the course content of the week, answered students' questions, shared and discussed several students' discussion posts, and provided review for the next learning topics in her weekly check-in video (see Fig. 1).

In addition to providing video feedback to the class, the instructional designer suggested using visual images summarizing types of interaction between course participants. The instructor included students' interactions among themselves in a visual format (see Fig. 2). These images helped students to understand how they were connected with each other in the discussion forums and encouraged them to expand their communications.

To evaluate the effectiveness of the instructional strategies and technologies implemented in this class, an end of class survey was administered. Eighteen of 20 students completed the survey (90% response rate). The quantitative portion, yielded positive feedback about the use of multimedia to promote learning. The qualitative part of the survey asked students to share their interdisciplinary group learning experience through five open-ended questions. Three themes emerged.

First, a genuine and authentic learning community was born! Most students shared positive experiences and attitudes toward the interdisciplinary learning setting. A student

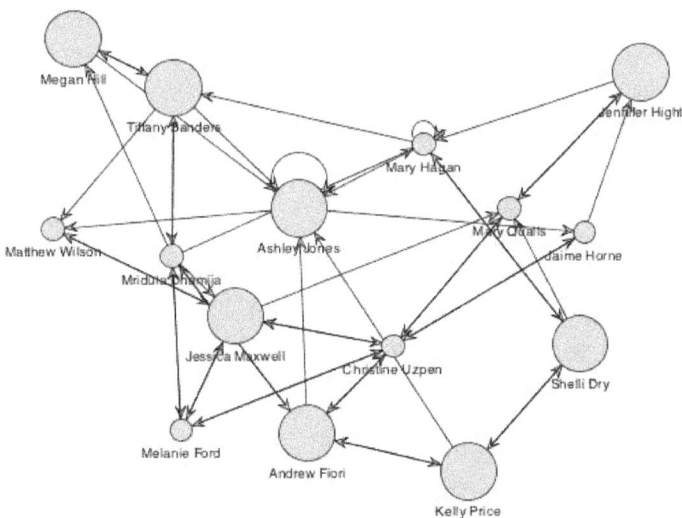

Figure 2: Students' interaction within the discussion board forum.

indicated "I learned that everyone is different, even if you are in the same discipline. This just means we can all help each other out in the field with our different ideas."

Second, first-hand experience of critical thinking in the online environment was evident. The interdisciplinary group setting exposed students to different ways of thinking or approaches toward the same issue presented, which challenged the students to re-evaluate their own way of thinking. One student's feedback perfectly reflects the critical thinking spirit in the class – "It is amazing how great minds truly do think alike. While each team offered slightly different perspectives or focused on other main points than my team, it was always refreshing to know we were all on the same page when it comes to wanting what is best for a student. I also thought it was interesting how each team had the same assignment descriptions and rubrics; however, formatted their pages and formulated goals/interventions differently. This just goes to show that this is not one right or wrong way to implement our related services as long as we are utilizing professional resources and evidence to guide our thinking."

Third, student commitment and engagement in an online learning environment was promoted. While students appreciated the convenience of online learning, they also indicated time commitment was one of the factors that prevented them from having good learning experiences in this class. Nevertheless, they indicated this class had helped them to become more effective learners. One student stated: "I learned I needed to be a more effective communicator with others. Often other professionals did not know what our roles and responsibilities were...."

While most students' learning experiences in this class were positive, negative feedback was identified as it impacted online learning. Several students stated that the learning management system (i.e., Blackboard) was not easy to use and the structure of blogging made it difficult for them to follow their peers' comments.

The course design provided multiple opportunities for students to interact. It is apparent in students' feedback that the multiple venues of interpersonal communication facilitated engagement. The weekly check-in videos helped students to see each other's relationships and reinforced the value of a learning community.

Finally, we want to emphasize that no technologies would automatically create rich and meaningful learning experiences without effective course design and delivery strategies. A collaborative partnership between the instructor and instructional designer and the participation and effort from the students themselves is paramount.

References

Garrison, D. R., Anderson, T., & Archer, W. (2001). Critical thinking, cognitive presence, and computer conferencing in distance education. *American Journal of Distance Education, 15*(1), 7–23.

Hattie, J. & Timperley, H. (2007). The power of feedback. *Review of Educational Research, 77*(1), 81-112.

Loureiro-Koechlin, C., & Allan, B. (2010). Time, space and structure in an e-learning and e-mentoring project. *British Journal of Educational Technology, 41*(5), 721-735.

Smyth, R. (2011). Enhancing learner–learner interaction using video communications in higher education: Implications from theorising about a new model. *British Journal of Educational Technology, 42*(1), 113-127

Wanju Huang, Purdue University
Shirley O'Brien, Eastern Kentucky University

How to Provide Students with Amazing and Awesome Feedback

I [Annie] am a student, not a professor. This perspective enables me to share some advice on how to provide students with constructive feedback on assignments. I wrote this essay because I have had both wonderful and miserable experiences with professors' feedback. The most useful feedback I received was from professors who gave me specific suggestions to improve an assignment *before* the final draft was due. The most useless feedback was illegibly scrawled cryptic notes, delivered months after the assignment was due, that consisted of platitudes like "Good job" or tersely worded messages of "Not your best work" with no specifics as to what I did well or what I did poorly. As I reflected on these experiences, I grew motivated to scour the SoTL literature to better understand the elements of good feedback—feedback that truly enables students to improve their skills and reach their goals.

The best research about student feedback has two elements in common: 1) It focuses on the student perspectives of helpfulness; and 2) It focuses on how feedback improves learning or performance on the skill itself. Consistent with the first of these best practices, a 2008 study by Poulos and Mahony asked students what they consider to be critical components of good professor feedback. The students noted that timing is essential. The sooner after the exam or assignment the students received feedback, the more helpful they found it to be. Another factor that students mentioned was the perceived significance of the feedback. If students think the assignment and/or feedback is irrelevant to their future, they tend to ignore it. Students' developmental stage is also critical. Students who are in their first year of any program, be it undergraduate or graduate training, find feedback more important than more advanced students. Students also desire feedback that is consistent, clear, and transparent (such as with a rubric with point values).

Wiggins (2012) echoed the work of Poulos and Mahony, but added one more helpful suggestion by demonstrating the value of peer feedback. Students generally find peer feedback helpful because it allows them to receive more immediate feedback than if they wait on a professor to grade an assignment. To ensure that feedback is connected with a student's future goals, Wiggins suggests explaining to students how the assignment connects with their future goals and ensuring that the feedback given helps strengthen this connection. In addition to feedback that is consistent, clear, and transparent, Wiggins adds that feedback should be tangible, actionable, user-friendly, and ongoing. Tangible refers to feedback that is realistic given time and skill demands. Actionable feedback provides students with concrete steps to success to make good revisions. User-friendly feedback is not overwhelming as too much feedback at once, especially negative feedback, does not help students improve in the long fun. Finally, ongoing feedback provides multiple opportunities for students to apply what they have learned from previous assignments or experiences.

Although student perceptions about feedback are important, the gold standard in research on feedback focuses on the direct impact of feedback on student learning. Fluckiger, Vigil, Pasco, and Danielson (2010) examined this construct and found that feedback needs to focus on three critical aspects of learning. These aspects include 1) feedback on assignments, 2) feedback on the process (how it is done), and 3) feedback on progress made over time. To implement three-pronged feedback, professors are encouraged to use a "three color quiz." With the three color quiz approach, students take a quiz in three parts. The first part of the quiz is completed individually. A student answers all of the questions she/he knows in black ink. The second part of the quiz is group work, in which students work together in groups to answer questions the whole group or some of the group did not know. These answers are written in green ink. The third part consists of each student looking up any problematic remaining questions in their textbook. These answers are written in blue ink.

Did the three color quiz impact student learning? Fluckiger, Vigil, Pasco, and Danielson found that 95% of students who took the three color quiz were more satisfied with their learning than in a traditional individual quiz format. Test anxiety was also reduced in that 79% of students felt less nervous taking a three color quiz than a traditional one. More importantly, 90% of students who had questions about the material reported that they were clarified by the end of the quiz. Additionally, 84 percent of the students looked up the answers to questions they did not know after the three color quiz vs. 37 percent of students who took a traditional closed book quiz. Looking up the correct answer after a quiz is highly correlated with student learning.

Finally, Fluckiger, Vigil, Pasco, and Danielson advise professors to take the time to conference with their students in individual meetings. Specifically, they note that student learning in the class can be enhanced when professors conduct a midterm student conference with each student to discuss student strengths and weaknesses, as well as offer suggestions for improvement. When conferences occur mid-semester, students have time to apply the feedback they received rather than waiting to receive feedback at the end of the semester when it was too late to improve. Professors also found the midterm conference to be a good rapport builder.

Because feedback is so critical to student learning, investing some extra time in crafting effective and well-timed feedback pays great dividends for students. Providing such feedback is a hallmark of truly great professors.

References

Fluckiger, J., Vigil, Y. T., Pasco, R., & Danielson, K. (2010). Formative feedback: Involving students as partners in assessment to enhance learning. *College Teaching, 58,* 136-140.

Poulos, A. & Mahony, M. J. (2008). Effectiveness of feedback: the students' perspective. *Assessment and Evaluation in Higher Education, 33*(2), 143-154.

Wiggins, G. (2012). Seven keys to effective feedback. *Feedback for Learning, 70*(1), 10-16.

Annie Baumer, Spalding University
DeDe Wohlfarth, Spalding University

Designing Online Faculty Development to Facilitate SoTL

As we have developed our university's Teaching & Learning Innovation (TLI) series, which offers in-person workshops for faculty from all colleges across campus, a small group of committed faculty and administrators have designed a new online system for the campus community. The DEEP (Developing Excellence in Eastern's Professors) system, developed by the **Faculty Innovation Workgroup**, advances faculty and professional development at Eastern Kentucky University (EKU) through the integration of technology and resources that raises the profile of faculty teaching and scholarship.

As one example of an effort to develop online resources for faculty, DEEP represents an ongoing commitment to excellence among EKU faculty and an investment in the continued enhancement of teaching and learning across campus.

DEEP involves multiple levels that contain materials and assignments for successful completion:
- Learner
- Practitioner
- Advocate
- Scholar.

Signifying an intensified engagement in the pedagogical topic, each level is identified by learning outcomes and cognitive process dimensions outlined in the Revised Bloom's Taxonomy. The system is composed of content that is freely available online (open) and content that is available upon faculty login (closed). See http://studio.eku.edu/DEEP for a full description of the DEEP system at EKU.

Rationale: Why Take SoTL Faculty Development Online?

Faculty members are busy, and many of our most productive colleagues are also serving on multiple committees and leading major university initiatives. The DEEP system offers faculty members the opportunity to access materials in any place or space.

When the Faculty Innovation Workgroup surveyed faculty across campus, SoTL emerged as one of the topics of interest and a priority for development. The experience of developing SoTL content for the DEEP system has provided concepts that are applicable in many institutional contexts:
- Provide content that help faculty to link teaching and learning with research methods and protocol
- Organize material, modules, or courses to build on teaching experience to then include classroom-based research
- Focus content on intentional strategies for SoTL research that are planned in advance.

Designing Your SoTL Project

These prompts are intended to help you consider aspects of faculty SoTL projects. Outcomes can take the form of a research study, development of a campus initiative, or a document that explains or advocates for SoTL. Adapt or reuse these questions and prompts as you design faculty development programs focused on SoTL.

What is the "theme" of your SoTL project? Does it fit into a predefined area (or not)?

Research/Data Collection: _____

Scholarly Publication/Presentation: _____

Institutional Documentation/Document: _____

Faculty/Professional Dev Materials: _____

Why are you pursuing your SoTL project? Is there a problem that you hope to solve as a result of doing your SoTL project? If so, how will your project lead to a solution?

Identify your approach to this SoTL project. What information do you need to gather? How much time will it take to gather?

Information	Timeline

Identify the audience for your SoTL project. Who is your target audience? What are their feelings toward SoTL? How much do they know about SoTL?

How will you determine if your SoTL project is successful? How will the campus community determine if your SoTL project is successful?

What complications or barriers do you foresee in designing (and then delivering) your SoTL project?

What impact will your SoTL project have on faculty at EKU?

What impact will your SoTL project have on students at EKU?

Rusty Carpenter, Eastern Kentucky University
Shirley O'Brien, Eastern Kentucky University

Guide on the Side in the Form of a Text Message

Using technology within the classroom to improve student engagement has become ubiquitous within discourse amongst higher education faculty. Concurrently, using mobile devices has increased amongst the student body. The merging of these two would seem logical; however, it is a task that must be treaded upon lightly because using the device in class can easily take a student off task. Therefore, I propose using mobile technology as a means of communicating with students outside the class.

Faculty have become adept at using email and using the email function within the chosen LMS of the higher education institution. However, students are likely not to read the full message of the email. Students today are targeted consumers and can become engulfed in emails sent by marketing agencies; thus, our emails may be buried in the inbox. Truong (2010) found, "Text messaging has overtaken not just e-mail but also instant messaging in popularity. Ninety-seven percent of students use text messages as their main form of communication, as opposed to 30 percent for e-mail and 25 percent for instant messaging" (para. 3).

Over the years I noticed, students were coming to class unprepared. Students confessed that they were not checking their emails and they were not regularly checking announcements or updates on the LMS. For years, I would joke and tell students that if I sent them a text, then they would read it. Many students, admitted that a text would be most helpful. Then, I found an app for that very purpose. I can text students from a phone number that was not my personal number. Several of these apps now exist and are of no cost. A simple Internet search with the key words "school messaging app" will find you a few of the top rated ones.

Once I found the app, I had to develop a policy statement for my syllabus:

> As a courtesy, the instructor may text you information about the class. The instructor will **NOT** text deadlines for assignments or tests. The instructor will **NOT** text you directions for assignments. It is the student's responsibility to check the syllabus and Blackboard (LMS) for information. The instructor may send texts regarding changes in the syllabus, changes in the schedule, or class delays due to weather.
> It is optional for you to receive texts about the class. You must choose to opt-in.

I began texting students approximately three years ago. Sometimes the text would simply state, "Check your email" or "Stop by my office to pick up your graded projects." I noticed that a few minutes after the text was sent, students were logging in to the LMS or they would stop by my office. While this strategy worked very well within the upper-level courses, the first-year students were not logging in to the LMS as frequently or checking emails as diligently as the upper-level students. I realized that the first-year students were not as experienced with self-discipline as the upper-level students. Thus, I had to change how I used the texts within the lower-level courses. The dilemma became how do I provide them with information to prepare them for class, but not enable them to become dependent on checking email and the LMS only if they received a text?

Timing and brevity are key when sending a text. As much as I like to fantasize that students are pouring over their textbook and taking copious notes several days in advance to prepare for my class, students have reported that they do not think about the class until the night before or even hours just prior to the onset of class. Therefore, sending a text within a 24 hour time frame of the class time seems to be the optimal window. Sending students a "preview" of the upcoming class activities and giving them a brief assignment assists the first year students' understanding of the expectations of higher education. Short text messages allow the instructor to "chunk" the material into a "scannable" piece of information that points students to the larger document.

In my experience, I have found that using a simple "low tech" communication technique has made a great impact on assisting students in coming to class prepared. Although texts can appear to be impersonal, students enjoy receiving the reminder and believe it is personable. A simple text can help build that relationship with students, because at some level the faculty member has taken time to text them on their personal mobile device.

There are several apps on the market. I have chosen one that is easy to use and has several valuable features. First, it has a privacy feature. The students do not have my personal cell phone number, nor does the app provide me or other users with the student's personal phone number. The students have to "opt in" to use it. The students send a text to sign up for the service, and I simply tell them what message to text and where to send the message. Second, the app allows me to decide if the communication is one way or if the student can respond to the text. Third, I have the ability to text group messages or individual messages. Fourth, students can text each other within the app. Fifth, I can prewrite text messages and schedule automatic delivery on a predetermined date. Last, text messages can be sent via my computer or my mobile device.

Faculty compete with others for our students' time and attention. It is imperative to keep our class within their mind's eye because "Out of sight means out of mind." Texting is an easy way to communicate with students that has a very low learning curve for the user and can be implemented immediately. However, beware not to bombard the student with text communication as then we run the risk of their filtering out the information or opting out of the service.

Reference

Truong, K. (2010, June 17). Student smartphone use doubles; instant messaging loses favor. Wired Campus. Retrieved from http://chronicle.com/blogs/wiredcampus/student-smartphone-use-doubles-instant-messaging-loses-favor/24876

Mary A. Sciaraffa, Eastern Kentucky University

The Graphical Gradebook

I come from a very technical background, where research comes from laboratory experiments or computer modeling. Making the shift to the scholarship of teaching and learning hasn't been an easy one for me.

One location where "data collection" is almost automatic is an instructor's course gradebook. I keep mine in a spreadsheet, which makes it easy to manipulate data. The graphing tools in most spreadsheet programs are excellent and make it easy to see trends that can be discussed in a journal article.

An extension of the graphical gradebook is the use of *online* gradebook monitoring from a learning management system (LMS). It has been shown that online gradebook monitoring by the students is a significant positive predictor of final course grades (Geddes 2009). LMS data on how often and when students access gradebooks, assignments, solutions, and supplemental materials can be used in a similar manner as gradebook data.

You can plot the correlation between various grades, such as participation and final grade. For example, plot the grade from exam 1 versus that from exam 2 for each student. Typically, if a student does well on one exam, he/she scores well on another exam; the dots typically plot along a diagonal line at a 1:1 slope. Since I started giving an extra exam in week 2 of the course and then teaching the students how to study and do homework for learning, the variability between exam 1 and the rest of the exams is enormous. The correlation between the other exams has much less variability. Does this result show that my instruction in studying works? Can this data be used to identify students who are actually using the study techniques? Time will tell when I get more data points.

Reference

Geddes, D., (2009). "How am i doing? Exploring on-line gradebook monitoring as a self-regulated learning practice that impacts academic achievement." *Academy of Management Learning & Education, 8*(4), 494-510.

Anthony J Lamanna, Eastern Kentucky University

Reducing the Digital Divide at the Organizational Level

SoTL research presents us with a major problem. By definition, it focuses on the assessment of the students in our classrooms, asking important questions about how they learn best. However, students of color are overwhelmingly underrepresented in our college classrooms (Rivkin, 2016). Therefore, we should have questions about the generalizability of this research to the diverse classroom of the future. This essay will provide some suggestions to manage the "digital divide" in on-line classes in an effort to take steps so that our college classrooms and, by extension, our SoTL research mirror the beautiful racial, socio-economic and cultural diversity of our world.

The digital divide refers to the idea that students of color and students of lower socio-economic status typically have highly uneven familiarity with and access to computer resources. Most notably, students from affluent, urban white families typically have more access to resources than other students. This divide is due, in large part, to prior access (Chen, 2013). While we believe that offering training to students in how to use our learning management systems, such as Blackboard and Moodle, will bridge this gap, this philosophy is based on faulty logic because it does not consider the effects of social capital, the idea that not all students have access to the same resources, and that students selectively share their resources (Chen, 2013). Specifically, groups who have access to resources (primarily white and middle class students) are more likely to share their resources within their own group, perpetuating the current disparity (Chen, 2013). Thus, classroom racial segregation, which occurs for many societal reasons, creates artificial barriers for students of color and deepens the disparity of digital divide.

Reducing these disparities in the classroom can be difficult, yet reducing them in online learning presents entirely separate obstacles. With the digital divide, the assets in question may include knowledge to utilize resources, access to equipment, or stability of Internet access (Ayanso, Cho, & Lertwachara, 2014; Braverman, 2016). While access to equipment and stability of the Internet require national changes, improving knowledge can, and should, begin at the organizational level, at universities and colleges. The changes, however, require us to be aware of the problem and directly address it. As a concrete description of this problem, one student in an online class Michael taught could access Wi-Fi and a computer only from 4-8 p.m. on Sunday evenings at her church, where she went to work on her assignments for the week with her three young children in tow, doing her best to entertain them while doing her homework. This four-hour window was the only opportunity she had for the week to access the posted material, review podcasts, participate in discussion forums, and take exams. Students with home computers, laptops, and 24-hour accessible Wi-Fi obviously had a big advantage over this student in terms of access to the course material.

Sharing and Creating Resources

One strategy for reducing the digital divide is to identify students' current technological resources as early as possible in the semester. For instance, some students from a disadvantaged background may have limited access to digital media due to slow Internet connections, limited data plans, or the lack of access to technology beyond their cell phones (Stočes, Masner, & Jarolímek, 2015). As educators, we are at risk to assume that students' reduced number of postings, hastily completed homework, or poor performance on exams reflects their lack of motivation, studying, intelligence, or academic skills. In fact, the situation may reflect only technological knowledge or access problems. In these contexts, educators can enhance students' education by providing resources in both digital and physical media (Stočes, Masner, & Jarolímek, 2015). For example, if an educator has a collection of handouts or worksheets online, printing copies of these resources and distributing them to the class would help meet students' needs.

This strategy is beneficial in two ways. As previously mentioned, such action provides access to documents that students might not otherwise be able to view (Stočes, Masner, & Jarolímek, 2015). However, it has the added benefit of reducing student anxiety. For students who do not access the Internet frequently, using online resources can be intimidating. Therefore, physical copies of essential course material can reduce anxiety and ensure students are able to learn in ways that they feel most comfortable (Stočes, Masner, & Jarolímek, 2015). Providing physical copies of course material can be challenging in geographically diverse on-line classrooms with some students living many miles away from our universities. However, creative and simple solutions, such as utilizing the US postal service, can help reduce the digital divide.

Training Modules

Educators can also reduce the digital divide through the use of training modules (Armenta, Serrano, Cabrera, & Conte, 2012). Through training modules, educators can help increase student competence and confidence for students with less experience in online learning. Skills that must be addressed include helping students learn to navigate the computer and the online classroom. As students become more proficient in these skills, they will feel more comfortable utilizing online aids, which can lead to improved success in later education (Armenta, Serrano, Cabrera, & Conte, 2012).

Importantly, these techniques have the added benefit of distributing social capital among students, who will then transmit their knowledge to their cultural group. With this dispersion of knowledge, the digital divide and social capital can be reduced within a community, providing better advantages for students who may not have had them in the past. The national barriers to reducing the digital divide persist, including the lack of Internet connectivity in rural and other areas and problems accessing high quality technological equipment due to cost. However, our responsibility is to ensure a level playing field for all students in terms of access, knowledge, confidence, and resources by changing the status quo. Without such active efforts on our behalf, we will continue to perpetuate the digital divide (Maddison & Lõrincz, 2003, Sein & Furuholt, 2012).

References

Armenta, A., Serrano, A., Cabrera, M., & Conte, R. (2012). The new digital divide: The confluence of broadband penetration, sustainable development, technology adoption and community participation. *Information Technology for Development, 18*(4), 345. doi:10.1080/02681102.2011.625925

Ayanso, A., Cho, D. I., & Lertwachara, K. (2014). Information and communications technology development and the digital divide: A global and regional assessment. *Information Technology for Development, 20*(1), 60-77. doi:10.1080/02681102.2013.797378

Braverman, B. (2016). The digital divide. *Literacy Today (2411-7862), 33*(4), 16

Chen, W. (2013). The implications of social capital for the digital divides in America. *Information Society, 29*(1), 13-25. doi:10.1080/01972243.2012.739265

Maddison, S., & Lõrincz, G. (2003). Bridging the digital divide. *Computing & Control Engineering, 14*(1), 26.

Rivkin, S. (2016). Desegregation since the Coleman Report. *EducationNext, 16* (2).

Sein, M. K., & Furuholt, B. (2012). Intermediaries: Bridges across the digital divide. *Information Technology for Development, 18*(4), 332-344.

Stočes, M., Masner, J., & Jarolímek, J. (2015). Mitigation of social exclusion in regions and rural areas: E-learning with focus on content creation and evaluation. *Agris On-Line Papers in Economics & Informatics, 7*(4), 143-150.

Michael Daniel, Spalding University
DeDe Wohlfarth, Spalding University

VI. My SoTL Project

In the years since the publication of the first book in the "It Works for Me" series, *It Works for Me: Shared Tips for Teaching* (1998), we've received much feedback—some oral and some contained in emails. Our favorite response by far runs along the lines of "Thanks for the tips; I tried X and Y" since the writers took us up on our suggestion to use the book "as a ready reference tool, pulling from its tips, techniques, and assignments and tailoring them to fit your unique style and situation" (p. x). In short, merely reading a book of practical tips denies you the full benefits of the process. Why not try to implement a few suggestions? Why not apply someone else's thinking to a class of yours?

Unfortunately, we have never done a follow-up survey to determine how many readers have successfully or unsuccessfully applied an idea read about (sounds like a good SoTL project in itself), so with our tenth book in the series, we're trying something new. At its end, we're suggesting you use this book as an inspiration/launching pad to get started on a SoTL project of your own. We are going to provide you with a process that we guarantee if you follow it, you will produce a SoTL article, whether it's your first or fiftieth. Doing such a project could:

- Recharge your batteries
- Allow you to collaborate with colleagues or students
- Enhance your teaching and perhaps that of your campus and beyond
- Provide you with the necessary publications for promotion, tenure, or merit while allowing you to start to carve out a scholarly niche
- Increase student learning.

The Importance of Discipline

One warning comes first. As we have suggested in all our books that involve writing and research, whether creative or critical, you must have one quality to succeed—**DISCIPLINE**. Without it, your work will be at best sporadic. So what do we mean by discipline? In general, it's the determination or will to work. Specifically, we've found discipline in writing and research, like your New Year's resolution to get on a regular plan of exercise, necessitates four items:

A Daily Writing Goal: convince yourself that you will write X amount of words per day of scholarship. Start with something simple such as 500 words/two double-spaced, typed pages and gradually build up.

- **A Daily Place to Write**: Having a home office helps, even if it's just a card table for your research and laptop set up in a corner of the most unused room in the house, the dining room. Let everyone know that is your space.
- **A Daily Time to Write**: Ten percent of us are morning larks, and another ten percent are night owls. Whichever you are, that's the best time to write. On the other hand, some of us have to steal a moment before the kids awake or after they've gone to sleep.
- **A Commitment to Excellence**: Don't go through the motions in order to say, "I'm a writer." Become a writer striving for that short period every day to do your best.

The Ten-Step Process of SoTL

All good writing is a disciplined process that follows several steps. Here is a synthesis from what experience and research have taught us.

Step One: Be Aware

Our long-time readers probably realize that we believe the best piece of advice on writing, in fiction and non-fiction, comes from Henry James. In his "The Art of Fiction," James emphasizes the importance of the writer's being an active observer of life: "Try to be one of those people on whom nothing is lost." In a similar vein, in *Achieving Excellence in Teaching* (2014) we emphasize the importance of a cognitive filter we call "the scholarly frame of mind." Cultivating this filter means that you are more aware of potential research opportunities. When you see an item on TV, notice it in social media, find it in the daily news, or spot it while doing something apparently alien to scholarship, your mind tags that item as important. Stephen King claims his best story germs occur when two events overlap. Such a synthesis occurred for us, as we chronicled in an earlier chapter, when a new book by the Heath brothers was suddenly seen through the prism of classroom organization.

Step Two: Become an Active Collector

When these key germs come to you, find a way to make them stay. When we were getting started, we kept a folder literally labelled IDEAS in which we dropped notes about observations and perceptions, photocopies, and even actual articles we tore out of newspapers and magazines. Now the folder, thanks to Rusty's tutelage, is more electronic. When Hal and Charlie left teaching for administration, they ended up throwing out a "shark box" (the lawyers' term for the great white icon on the boxes) of potential pieces of literary criticism as well as folders of starts to articles. For years they even let their students hungry for a term paper/article idea scrounge through the collections to kick start production.

Step Three: Reflect in Writing Often

Writing a book on metacognition last year was easy because reflecting is a habit we continually practice. On Mondays we write a weekly post for New Forums' "Welcome Scholars" blog. What makes the writing easy is that our fingers on the computer keyboard are constantly trying to figure out why we do some things. For instance, on the very day Charlie was typing out a draft of this chapter, he wrote a post about how even though we are underfunded and do so without enough hours in the day, we keep adding services for our center for teaching and learning (CTL). To figure out why we keep stretching ourselves and our organization so thin, we wrote a post that came up with two good reasons. Charlie and Rusty prefer to reflect on the computer, while Hal works best in a semi-dark room with a pen and a notepad. In any case, for us reflection is a continuous process.

Step Four: Read the Literature

Right beside your favorite chair or sitting on your computer, is there an article you've saved and are dying to read? The most productive scholars also read—lots. Rusty, for instance, constantly forwards us material he has read. Charlie finds books mentioned in other sources such as the *Wall Street Journal* and orders them, and every morning when he comes in, Hal places something to read on Charlie's desk. Importantly, much of the reading results in reflection, discussion, and, ultimately, publication.

Step Five: Create Questions and Formulate Problems to Solve

Cox, Huber, and Hutchings (2004) report that in the Carnegie Academy for the Scholarship and Learning (CASTL), 81% of these scholars state that "I had questions about my students' learning that I wanted to explore." Obviously most of us come up with daily questions and problems about our teaching and student learning. Don't waste a terrific opportunity by letting these questions/problems drift away amidst the day's activities. Write them down for later, more focused consideration.

Step Six: Perform Market Research

We almost never write a piece for which we haven't previously determined a market. A few years ago we started reading the *National Teaching & Learning Forum* and saw it that as an excellent publication and an obvious market. A quick analysis determined that several people were writing 1600-word columns for editor James Rhem. At the time we were writing an *Introduction to Applied Creative Thinking* (2012) and developing a minor in Applied Creative Thinking, so we decided to play to our strengths and proposed a four times per year column we called "Creativity Café." We're still writing the column.

Over the years we've determined our best work is performed for sources we know. What do you read? Analyze the types of subjects, lengths, and other characteristics in those journals. Check out the articles published in that journal for their sources as possible targets for your writing. In "A 'Best of' List that Celebrates the Scholarship of Teaching & Learning," Weimer (2015) lists her eight top articles on SoTL, but more importantly enumerates the six characteristics that make them top:

- "about an innovative instructional approach that addresses a common learning need and is proven to work, either documented by research or supported by related research.
- A well-designed study on a topic we don't know a lot about, or a review of research or literature on a topic where our knowledge is much deeper. The review integrates what is known in ways useful to practitioners.
- A well-written exploration of a familiar topic that offers new insight.
- A provocative essay that challenges current thinking on a topic.
- A creative, intellectually rigorous example of scholarly work on teaching and learning.
- Relevant and widely applicable, something almost any teacher will find interesting and useful."

Do any of Weimer's descriptors either suggest something to you or describe something about which you've been reflecting?

Craig Nelson also suggests a typology of SoTL research you could perform:
1. Group 1: Reports on Particular Classes
   A. It worked!
   B. Before & After: Qualitative Assessments of Changes in Practice
   C. Before & After: Quantitative Assessments of Changes
2. Group 2: Reflections on Years of Teaching Experience Implicitly or Explicitly Informed by Other SoTL
   D. Essays Developing Good Ideas

E. Summaries of Expert Knowledge Gained by Self-Reflection and Experimentation in One's Own Teaching
   F. Integration of Larger Frameworks with Classroom Practice
3. Group 3: Larger Contexts: Comparisons of Courses & Comparisons of Student Change Across Time
   G. Qualitative Studies Designed to Explore a Key Issue
   H. Quantitative Comparisons of Different Courses or Comparisons
   I. Comparisons of a Wide Array of Different Courses Using a Common Assessment Instrument
4. Group 4: Formal Research
   J. Experimental Analysis
5. Group 5: Summaries and Analyses of Sets of Prior Studies
   K. Annotated Bibliographies
   L. Brief, Annotated Summaries of Key Research Findings
   M. Formal (Quantitative Meta-Analyses)

Surely, in Nelson's taxonomy of SoTL research, something has jumped out that interests you.

Step Seven: Determine a Research Methodology

Research methodology is a formidable-sounding term, but it needn't be. Here are a few simple suggestions.

Our best advice is to *begin with a methodology with which you are familiar.* In English, for instance, a literature review means something different from how social and natural scientists utilize it. Moreover, certain fields favor certain approaches. In general, all the sciences tend to be based on quantitative research, while the arts and humanities employ mostly qualitative research because their graduate curricula have not necessitated the taking of a course in statistics.

Pick the low-hanging fruit. Begin with a survey. If you have trouble coming up with a five-to-ten-question survey, get help from your campus' institutional research division. If you find you have to use statistics, collaborate with someone in that field. Learn how you can use the same survey as both a pre-test and post-test. If you teach two sections of the same course, try doing something different in one of the classes, then seeing if you can figure out a common test that you can use to demonstrate increased learning resulted from one approach. Other simpler approaches are focus groups, observations, questionnaires, and even thematic reviews. Our biggest problem with even low-hanging fruit was trying to figure out the minimum number of subjects—i.e., the n—needed, which is why Institutional Research is on our speed dial.

Choose a subject that interests you. If quizzing at the beginning of class is something you've always believed in, test your own assumption. If you can't figure out whether a quiz works better than a reflection, try doing one in each of your two sections. We wrote a SoTL piece about the relationship between coaching and teaching because we were also coaching on the high school level, and we developed another article on total team teaching because that was the way we always taught our creative writing graduate classes.

Piggyback off extant lit. Remember our telling you about how we developed the C.R.I.S.P. approach to classroom organization? Why don't you test the idea in your classes? Or, maybe you like Gerry Nosich's belief in emphasizing "fundamental and powerful concepts" in the classroom. Well, it's another theory that lends itself to the two-section approach.

Experiment with one of the approaches in Nelson's taxonomy. Notice his first idea is "It worked!" Doesn't that sound a lot like our series of practical teaching tips for New Forums under the general title of "It Works for Me"? Maybe your forte is simply summarizing the research on a subject such as total team teaching.

Step Eight: Analyze the Data/Research

This step can be complicated, or you can make it simpler by avoiding the data part. In the previous step, you might go beyond a list of books and articles on total team teaching and actually analyze the research for common themes. In so doing, you might find that certain elements of the subject have been neglected. Maybe you pinpoint something crucial on which disagreement reigns (if you're really good, you might proffer a hitherto not-thought-of solution).

But if you work with data and feel insecure, we're hopeful you collaborated with someone on creating the data. If so, this person is probably knowledgeable about how to analyze it. Don't forget: collaboration is a valuable tool in scholarship of any sort.

Step Nine: Write and Rewrite the Article

Eventually you must write. When we taught creative writing, we used to drill in our students the circular definition that a writer is one who writes . . . often. Writing is a muscle that must be exercised daily. Our daily habit has us writing around a thousand words per day seven days a week. Much like the athlete who becomes more comfortable and productive with a regular number of "reps," so you will increase both the quantity and quality of your work through constant practice. Our experience has shown that, in addition, regular writing sessions make the scholarly process much less daunting and open to procrastination or omission.

Where and when you write makes little difference as long as you are regular and consistent. Charlie, for instance, likes to sit at a large desk in either his office or at home where he can sprawl the research out in front of him. He has already marked up the pieces and jotted down a vague outline. He finds that the computer has basically doubled his output. Quality has increased as he can pause to go online to immediately check a detail, go back to a source's source, or even fine tune by looking up what key terms mean. In a first draft, whenever an idea strikes him, he types it out. Just now the idea of "rejection" dropped into his mind, so he dropped down to Step Ten and typed the word in as a reminder of something to pick up later. Revision is the process of making sense of drafts. While having their own regimens, Hal and Rusty also have established regularity in their writing—each writing in a fashion that fosters productivity.

And, of course, collaborations like ours demand that we constantly send out what we have written to each other and incorporate changes.

But, truthfully, we never start to write cold. On our way to and from the office (Hal and Charlie walk; Rusty drives), we pre-compose in our heads. Sitting at the computer or scribbling on a legal pad or even napkin becomes a way of letting the writing out.

Step Ten: Submit the Article

Since every piece we do is written with a specific market in mind, the final step of submission is an easy one. Knowing our market means we have checked out a journal's editorial requirements before we start, and if Calibri 12 is demanded, that's what we use. We stay under word counts and use the called-upon style guides. A very influential editor once told us that she received so many submissions that she used her first read-through to cull out those manuscripts that did not follow her well-publicized requirements.

Submitting also means resubmitting. If we receive a revise and resubmit recommendation, we do what we're asked. If, as happens often, we find reviewers disagreeing, we ask the editor to arbitrate. If we are rejected, we usually check our sources' publication spots and then survey those markets to determine alternate submission sites. Before sending off the manuscript, we make sure we have covered any question/concerns advanced by the reviewers and the editor of the journal that originally rejected the piece. Since no article sitting on a jumpdrive has ever been accepted, we keep plugging away. At this moment, we are proud to report we have no rejected articles sitting in our revise pile . . . or our garbage can.

References

Cox, R., Huber, M. & Hutchings, P. (2004). *Survey of CASTL scholars*. Stanford, CA: The Carnegie Foundation for the Advancement of Teaching.

Nelson, C. (n.d.). How Could I Do Scholarship of Teaching & Learning? Retrieved 11 November 2016 from http://php.indiana.edu/~nelson1/SOTLGENRESS.html.

Weimer, M. (2015, January 7). A `best of' list that celebrates the scholarship of teaching & learning. *Faculty Focus*. http://www.facultyfocus.com/articles/teaching-professor-blog/best-list-celebrates-scholarship-teaching-learning

VII. The Future of SoTL

Every time we do a presentation on SoTL, we get a question along the lines of "Where do you think SoTL is headed?" Our answer is intertwined with where we think higher education is going.

While we have been writing this book, we have also been reading Berg and Seeber's *The Slow Professor* (2016), and while we disagree with some of their conclusions, we heartily concur with some of their premises. Due to the accountability movement, what they call "the corporate university" is more and more moving forward to the chant of the phrase "evidence-based." As the need for more and better evidence permeates every aspect of academia, we would be fools to think it won't affect SoTL.

Excellence in teaching will become increasingly what alumni donors and state legislatures support. SoTL will be forced to move up Weimer's continuum from wisdom-of-practice reflections to something resembling pure educational research. General theories will be challenged, and only those that support themselves with good data will flourish. Blogging, diaries, and "Look what I did" will slip down the acceptability charts. Articles on "Grail Imagery in Cheever's 'The Swimmer'" will become less important than "Using Cheever's 'The Swimmer' to Maximize Student Learning." Published SoTL articles are quantifiable and thus become the darlings of the accountability-minded overseers.

The Scholarship of Service will develop in a parallel fashion to SoTL, but because of its often civic-based nature enabling the building of an informed citizenry, that field of scholarship has a built-in advantage.

Scholars in both areas, though, will have to figure out how to apply SoTL to higher education idols such as assessment, strategic plans, curricula, and even diversity.

SoTL will progressively promote faculty-student collaborations in order to demonstrate the two bodies are co-facilitators of knowledge, a trait of teaching that increases life-long learning.

Formal SoTL is young. When it is twice as old as it is now, SoTL will be the dominant form of collegiate research. SoTL Centers will be as much a part of the campus scene as tech centers and administration centers (which will, no doubt, continue to balloon in hires).

Reference

Berg, M. & Seeber, B. (2016). *The slow professor*. Canada: University of Toronto Press.

About the Authors

Hal Blythe, Ph.D. (University of Louisville, 1972), is the Co-Director of the Teaching & Learning Center at Eastern Kentucky University. With Charlie, he has collaborated on over 1200 published works, including 25 books (ten in New Forums' popular It Works For Me Series), literary criticism, and educational research.

Charlie Sweet, Ph.D. (Florida State University, 1970), is the Co-Director of the Teaching & Learning Center at Eastern Kentucky University. With Hal, he has collaborated on over 1200 published works, including 25 books, literary criticism, educational research, and ghostwriter of the lead novella for the *Mike Shayne Mystery Magazine*.

Russell Carpenter, Ph.D. (University of Central Florida, 2009), is executive director the Noel Studio for Academic Creativity and Minor in Applied Creative Thinking at Eastern Kentucky University where he is also Associate Professor of English. He is the author or editor of several recent books including *The Routledge Reader on Writing Centers and New Media* (with Sohui Lee), *Cases on Higher Education Spaces*, *Teaching Applied Creative Thinking* (with Charlie Sweet, Hal Blythe, and Shawn Apostel), and the *Introduction to Applied Creative Thinking* (with Charlie Sweet and Hal Blythe). He serves as Past President of the Southeastern Writing Center Association and Editor of the *Journal of Faculty Development*.

The authors invite you to try their *Scaling the Scholarship Mountain* (New Forums Press), which is a companion piece to *It Works for Me with SoTL*.

www.ingramcontent.com/pod-product-compliance
Lightning Source LLC
Chambersburg PA
CBHW080452170426
43196CB00016B/2774